IN PRAISE OF
TEDDY BEAR

A Friend for life: Pip Miller with her Steiff bear, Teddy, in 1907
She still has him today.

IN PRAISE OF
TEDDY BEARS

Collector's Edition

———————

Philippa Waring

SOUVENIR PRESS

First published 1980 by Souvenir Press Ltd.,
43 Great Russell Street, London WC1B 3PA
and simultaneously in Canada

This edition, completely revised, reset and
redesigned, with new text and illustrations,
published 1997

ISBN 0 285 63410 0

Typeset by
Rowland Phototypesetting Limited, Bury St Edmunds,
Suffolk
Printed in Great Britain by
St Edmundsbury Press Limited, Bury St Edmunds, Suffolk

A teddy is soft and warm and inevitably becomes the father figure in the nursery. As people grow older and have to face worries, their teddy becomes the means of recapturing the serenity of childhood.

Carl Bruin
Psychiatrist, 1985

Of all the otherwise mundane objects which stir our collecting instinct, from cigarette cards to bottle tops, nothing provokes so much sentiment as the sight of an old battered teddy bear. The subject is such an emotional one that it is easy to overlook the fact that commercially Teddy has been the world's most successful toy.

Carol Ann Stanton
Antiques Historian, 1978

CONTENTS

PREFACE TO THE NEW EDITION

The first edition of this book was published on 23 October, 1980, as part of a special 'National Bear Awareness Week' campaign. One of the first books which helped to make the general public 'bear aware', it owed much to the support, encouragement and information supplied by three people all of whom, sadly, have since died; their role in generating the present worldwide interest in teddy bears is beyond dispute.

First, there was Lieutenant-Colonel T. R. 'Bob' Henderson, a retired British Army officer who had for years been interested in the influence of teddy bears on western society and in 1962 was nominated 'President of the Teddy Bear Club'. Second was James T. Ownby, an American journalist

Two arctophiles who attended the launching of the original edition of this book during National Bear Awareness Week in October 1980.

and charity worker, who in 1970 founded the Good Bears of the World organisation, dedicated to presenting teddies to sick children and adults as well as uniting teddy bear enthusiasts all over the world. The third was Peter Bull, the ebullient English actor who in 1969 published his very personal memoir, *Bear With Me*, which gave the earliest hint of the growing circle of dedicated teddy bear lovers and collectors. All three responded enthusiastically to my requests for help in preparing the first popular history of the teddy bear and his human admirers, and seventeen years later, in this new edition, I am pleased to have the opportunity to acknowledge my debt to them.

Colonel Bob died at his home in Edinburgh in 1990, having become a celebrity famed for his theories about the psychotherapeutical powers of teddy bears to generate comfort and security. Jim Ownby passed away in 1986, and when the Good Bears of the World organisation he had run from his home in Honolulu, Hawaii, was transferred to Ohio, it boasted more than 10,000 members and an annual 'Good Bear Day' which he had inaugurated on 27 October to celebrate Theodore Roosevelt's birthday with rallies throughout the world. Peter Bull died in London in 1984, knowing that his writings had helped to make love of teddy bears a perfectly respectable emotion for adults, although it had actually existed unacknowledged for years.

So much has happened in the years since 1980 that it was felt necessary to revise and expand some aspects of the book. Teddy bears have become so popular that there are now many shops, museums and magazines to cater for the growing market. In the field of collecting teddy bears are fetching at auction prices that would have been thought impossible even ten years ago, and there is a growing interest in teddy bear manufacturers and their histories, and in identifying the rarest and most collectable bears from each source. These trends have all been covered in this new edition, but I have also been able to include new information resulting from the publication of the first edition. Many people got in touch to tell me about their own teddy bears or about people connected with the history of bear awareness, and have allowed me to share their accounts and pictures with readers.

I am only sad that not one of the three generous-hearted men who started me on the trail is around now to see just what a phenomenon has developed in their wake. I am certain, however, that they would be pleased and proud, and it is with this in mind that I dedicate this new edition of *In Praise of Teddy Bears* to them all.

Philippa Waring
July 1997

1

A BEAR FOR ALL SEASONS

Ninety-five years ago, on 14 November, 1902, the teddy bear was born when American President Theodore Roosevelt, out on a hunting expedition, refused to shoot a bear cub, thereby inspiring a New York shopkeeper to produce a 'Teddy's Bear' to sell to children. That toy, made of honey-coloured plush, excelsior and boot button eyes, was the progenitor of all modern teddies and the beginning of a teddy bear craze that now circles the globe. It is a phenomenon that appeals to adults as much as to the children for whom the toys were originally intended. For the teddy bear, although it may ostensibly be no more than an appealing-looking combination of fabric, stuffing and artificial features, has won a unique place in the human heart as comforter, confidant and soulmate. It is at once a symbol of childhood and an expression of love

The famous phrase 'Teddy Bear's Picnic' has inspired songs, books and even cartoons! (*The Times*, 29 October, 1994).

between two people, and no other inanimate object has quite its appeal. Teddy has, with every justification I believe, been called the world's most popular soft toy—which is no mean achievement for such a newcomer to the world of playthings.

Those who love teddy bears are known as *arctophiles*, a term derived from the Greek *arktos*, meaning 'bear,' and *philos*, 'friend'. The word may sound a little offputting, but it simply refers to anyone who owns a teddy, collects them or just finds them irresistible. Indeed, in homes all over the world you will find a ragged old teddy which has survived a childhood of hugs and secrets and still sits in a special place of its own—

The author's 'hug' of bears, including a rare Schuco miniature.

12

most likely in the bedroom, because that is teddy's domain where he offers the most and demands the least. Who else will put up with being dragged around for years by one leg with his head bumping on the ground? Or, when you are older, will lend an ear to your worries about work, your failure to keep to a diet or even the secrets of your love life— all without yawning or letting his eyes glaze over? A teddy bear may be simply the best friend you will ever have.

People from all walks of life have cherished their teddy bears. The British royal family, for example, all have teddies: the Queen Mother still treasures an early Chad Valley bear, Lady Elizabeth, which was presented to her by the manufacturers, and Prince Charles apparently travels everywhere with his bear, Teddy, carefully stored in a shirt bag. Prince Andrew also has one, named Bruno, which was given to him by the actress Koo Stark. Several members of the aristocracy have owned up to hanging on to their old teddies, including the Duke of Westminster, Lord Romsey and the father of the present Marquess of Bath, whose bespectacled Clarence Chair Bear became something of a celebrity at the family home, Longleat, in Wiltshire. Baroness Thatcher's Humphrey wears blue dungarees and has regularly put in appearances at charity events, as has Sir David Steel's Beveridge who is never to be seen without his bright yellow Liberal Democrat rosette. People in the world of show business have their bears, too, including Richard Briers' Ragged, a rather threadbare chap after years of the good life; the late Jill Bennett's anarchic little friend Sir Teggy; Samantha Eggar's Mr Bear; and Dusty Springfield's supremely intelligent Mr Einstein. Even Pope John Paul is said to keep his childhood bear with him in the Vatican in Rome.

There are countless more less well-connected bears enjoying their retirement in ordinary homes up and down the country, probably recovering from their owners' younger days when

A rare sketch by E.H. Shepard, the illustrator of *Winnie-the-Pooh*, for A.A. Milne's short story, 'Miss Waterlow in Bed' (1939).

13

they were never allowed a moment's peace. In fact that is precisely where the bond begins, when a child takes out its emotions on teddy—ticking him off, feeding him and almost loving him to death. Dr Leonard Kristal, who made a study of the psychological value of the 'teddy bear, has explained his findings.

'Teddy bears spell comfort and security,' he says. 'They remind grown-ups of the happier times of their childhood. There's nothing threatening about them—they never yell back. And it is a comfort to have something around that's lived with you all your life—and still likes you! There is nothing wrong with teddies for adults.'

The late Colonel Bob Henderson, who helped in the writing of this book, had his own theory about 'Teddy Bear Consciousness', as he called it:

> During the first half of the twentieth century it was found that the subtle appeal of the teddy bear was so endearing and enduring that the teddy has become the lasting symbol of childhood, and consequently outlived all other mascot animals. It is not realised that anybody who thinks the teddy bear is just a cuddly toy and nothing more is very much mistaken. There is far more to teddy than meets the eye. For there is now ample evidence to show that the teddy bear gives solace and enjoyment to people of all ages and both sexes. So much so, in fact, that this takes it right out of the classification of a soft toy.

The influence of the teddy bear has also spread far beyond its status as a plaything. Teddies are to be found in advertising, as logos, and in high-profile promotions. (The Belgrave-Sheraton Hotel in London, for example, informs potential visitors that, 'Any VIP or child guest who's forgotten their bear essential may borrow one of our dozen resident teddies'.) They have had books, poetry, jokes and songs written about them—an annual 'Teddy Bears' Concert' is held in London at the Barbican—and they appear regularly in films, television and on radio. Teddies are popular features on postcards, greeting cards and in cartoons, as well as making ideal souvenirs. In the domestic world they can be found on foodstuffs, cleansers and just about any household product you care to name.

A teddy bear named Pudsey has come to symbolise the BBC's annual fund-raising appeal for Children in Need, while another couple of teds named Richard and Emma went round the world in the BT Global Challenge yacht race covering more than 48,000 kilometres (30,000 miles). As a lucky mascot

(*Opposite*) The famous Hollywood child star Shirley Temple was a great teddy bear fan and posed with them for numerous publicity photographs like this one.

14

An early German teddy bear with a 'bag' body and long 'sack' arms. This picture of a surviving example, named Hans, was sent to the author by his proud owner.

a teddy is said to be without peer, and the Russians chose one, Mishka, for the 1980 Moscow Olympic Games. Teddies also have their own entry in *The Guinness Book of Records*, marking the day in February 1993 when 9,750 turned up with their owners for the world's largest teddy bears' picnic in Auckland, New Zealand.

Teddy has even found a place in commerce. Talking bears in suits, white shirts and red ties, which encourage New York businessmen to do better by repeating the phrase, 'You're on your way to the top—you're a born leader', have become increasingly familiar sights alongside the photographs of wife and children in the offices of male company executives. For women aiming for the top there is a female bear in a red-striped blouse and white skirt, who will encourage them, 'Be what you want to be. You're perfect—just perfect!' In the City of London teddy bears are seen as good news for investors: in April 1997 the English Teddy Bear Company, which already has eleven shops in the UK, was able to raise capital funding to expand into America, Japan and Asia. The teddy bear has also earned its own spot on the Internet which gives details of forthcoming teddy events and information about teddy bear museums, shops and suppliers. There is even an option to send in a photo of your own bear with details. For those who might want to visit the site, the code is:

http://www.teddy-bear-uk.demon.co.uk.

Today teddy bears are hardly ever out of the news. After the terrible tragedy in Dunblane in March 1996, for example, hundreds of teddies were sent by children all over Britain as tokens of love and sympathy to the youngsters at the little Scottish town's primary school where sixteen of their friends had been gunned down. 'A Mountain of Teddy Bears in the

Taking care of teddy: a sketch from the medical treatise, *Some Observations on the Diseases of Brunus edwardii.*

School of Tears' was how *The People* headlined its story of 17 March. In the United States, a month later, it was reported that teddy bears were to be used in police cars at Morgan Hill, a community sixty miles from San Francisco in California, to mollify criminals and calm frightened children. 'I don't particularly care for guns,' said Mayor Lorraine Barke who came up with the idea. 'The teddy bear is a positive piece of equipment.' And at the Davidson County Jail in North Carolina it was reported in November 1996 that cells were being painted with teddy bears in an experiment to calm angry prisoners.

Here at home, miniature cameras have been designed to insert behind the eyes of teddy bears as a way of observing childminders, following a series of cases of abuse while parents were away from home. A group of scientists at Marconi in Scotland have designed a ted with a microphone concealed in its nose, which will activate its eyes to wink whenever a noise is made, so encouraging profoundly deaf children to make their first sounds. And in France psychologist Professor Marcel Rufo has advocated using teddy bears as teaching aids when preparing children for surgery. He has encouraged surgeons to spend time cutting and stitching the stomach of a little patient's bear before an operation; or if the teddy is old and ragged, repairing the hole and bandaging the toy. He even involves anaesthetists in the role-playing to demonstrate their techniques on the bear and then to put up the appropriate drips. According to Professor Rufo, 'Operation Teddy' has significantly hastened the recovery of many of his young patients. On a rather different medical note, a treatise exists on what makes teddies poorly! Called *Some Observations on the Diseases of Brunus edwardii (Species nova)* by D. K. Blackmore, D. G. Owen and C. M. Young, it appeared in *The Veterinary Record* in 1972 and was later reprinted as a booklet.

Perhaps the most extraordinary medical story of all occurred in October 1996, when the psychic Uri Geller was reported to have used his powers to heal US Vice-President Al Gore's six-year-old son, Albert, after he was hit by a car. Geller 'physically charged' a teddy bear and sent it to the child. According to the press, Albert 'made a quick recovery'.

A natural consequence of this growth of interest in teddy bears has been that they have become very collectable—and in some cases quite valuable—with the result that it is no longer the fate of most worn-out bears to be consigned to the dustbin: they are more likely to be taken to the nearest auction house or dealer. Always assuming that their pedigree is right, of course. It is worth remembering that the most sought-after bears are not necessarily those in pristine condition, for many collectors are much more interested in a threadbare teddy than one in perfect condition which has clearly never been loved. With this in mind I have added a new chapter to the book, offering some guidance about the leading teddy bear manufacturers, their most popular lines and the sort of prices these may fetch.

Even though the popularity of the teddy bear has increased so dramatically over the past twenty years, the relationship between a bear and its owner remains an intensely personal one. This feeling was neatly explained to me by Michael Bond, creator of Paddington Bear, another important figure in teddy history:

'Despite broken growls, noses hanging by the slenderest of threads, worn paws, and the occasional loss of an eye, they remain steadfast and true through thick and thin. They are there when wanted, but quite content to await your pleasure. It is an ideal recipe for the perfect friendship.'

I hope readers will appreciate that this book has not lightly been called *In Praise of Teddy Bears*. The history, development and international appeal of the bear make fascinating reading. At least that is what all those of us who are already arctophiles and our little companions truly believe.

A striking advertisement from the catalogue of the famous US firm Sears Roebuck, 1931.

2

THE TEDDY BEAR'S ANCESTORS

The bear is an older inhabitant of the Earth than man himself, and its great antiquity has undoubtedly contributed to its special place in folklore, myth and legend. Bearlike creatures roamed the world more than twelve million years ago, but it was not until something like one million years ago that the true bear appeared and was later named *Ursus* (the Latin for bear) to differentiate it from its predecessors.

Perhaps not surprisingly, the bear came to be worshipped by early peoples, and evidence has been found that Neanderthal man had a bear cult which elevated the giant cave bear of 75,000 years ago into a god. With the passage of time legends developed about bear gods and goddesses, and such stories are particularly prevalent among the North American Indians. One of the most widespread mythical ideas about bears was that their young were born as formless lumps which the mother bear then licked into the shape of tiny cubs. (They are actually very small, blind and hairless at birth.) This belief gave rise to the expression of a child being 'licked into shape' by its parents.

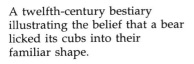
A twelfth-century bestiary illustrating the belief that a bear licked its cubs into their familiar shape.

Our modern bears fall into four main types, all belonging to the plantigrade mammals, so called because they walk on the whole sole of the foot, in contrast to the digitigrades, such as dogs and cats, which rest their weight only upon the toes or front part of the paws. Bears are found in nearly all parts of the world (with the exception of Australia which is the home of their relative, the koala) and it is well known that they never willingly attack human beings. These are the four types:

Polar Bear (*Thalarctos maritimus*) is found in the northern Arctic regions only and is one of the most handsome creatures in creation. It is the largest of all the bears, rarely less than 2.4 metres (8 feet) in length and sometimes as much as 3.4 metres (11 feet), and covered with beautiful yellowish-white fur. The polar bear is a great swimmer, very agile in the water, and can cover distances of up to forty miles at a stretch.

Grizzly Bear (*Ursus horribilis*) from the American continent is next in size to the polar bear, but surpasses it in strength and ferocity. Its fur varies in colour from light grey to blackish-brown, and the creature got its name 'grizzly' from the fact that this fur is either tipped with grey or shot through with grey hairs, giving it a grizzled effect.

Black Bear (*Ursus americanus*) is also a dweller of the American continent, but much smaller than the grizzly—usually about 1.5 metres (5 feet) long—and has smooth, black, glossy hair. The bear will attack small quadrupeds, but lives chiefly

German postcard of a black bear clearly showing the hump which was a feature of the early teddy bears, like this example from the Montgomery Ward catalogue of 1922.

20

The famous brown bear in typical pose and the restored head of a short-faced bear (*Arctotherium bonærense*), from the National Museum, Buenos Aires.

on berries and roots, although its great delight is eating honey and it will brave repeated stings to secure a honeycomb!

Brown Bear (*Ursus arctos*) is found over much of the world, in particular Europe, Russia, Asia and even Japan. Its hair is usually brown, but it can vary from almost black to virtually yellow. A solitary animal by nature, it has a rather good-humoured appearance created by its large eyes and pleasing expression. It can, though, hug its enemies to death in its strong embrace!

It should be mentioned that the bear family is related to the raccoon (Procyonidae) to which the panda (*Ailurus fulgens*) also belongs. The largest member of this group is the much admired giant panda (*Ailuropoda melanoleuca*). Here again *uro* like *arcto* means bearlike, and in China, where the creature lives, it is called 'beishung' meaning 'the white bear' and models of it are regarded as teddy bears. Likewise the koala from Australia is named *Phascolarctos cinereus*, the *arctos* being included because it is bearlike. In Australia it is called the 'tree bear' or native sloth, and models of it are referred to as the Australian teddy bear.

Bears have featured in romance and literature for centuries and have a special place in the folklore of several nations, in particular Russia where they are seen as almost man-like because of the way they walk upright. In many Russian stories the bear is depicted as 'friendly, hospitable, cheery, the best of comrades, the worst of officials, tolerant of all social vices, pitiless only to the pretentious', to quote Jane Harrison and Hope Mirrless in their *Book of the Bear* (1926).

For many people the most famous of bear stories is *The Three Bears*, widely believed to have been an old fable first written down by the English writer Robert Southey in his miscellany, *The Doctor*, published between 1834 and 1847. In

21

Sketch of the immortal 'Three Bears' by L. Leslie Brooke for a 1902 edition of the story.

fact there is a manuscript version of the story by Eleanor Mure, written at least three years earlier than Southey's. The work, bearing the title 'The Celebrated Nursery Tale of The Three Bears; put into verse and embellished with drawings for a Birthday Present to Horace Broke, September 26, 1831', is held in the Osbourne Collection of Early Children's Books housed in the Toronto Public Library. What is particularly interesting about the mysterious Mrs Mure's version (for we know absolutely nothing about her) is that it is an old woman and not a young girl who steals the bears' porridge and then falls asleep in their house. She also gives the tale an ending not found elsewhere, in which the bears discover the old woman and then punish her in a most heartless way:

One of the teddy bear's famous ancestors, 'Bre'r Bear', from *Uncle Remus* by Joel Chandler Harris, illustrated by J.A. Shepherd, 1902.

On the fire they throw her, but burn her they couldn't,
In the water they put her, but drown there she wouldn't;
They seize her before all the wondering people,
And chuck her aloft on St Paul's church-yard steeple;
And if she's still there when you earnestly look,
You will see her quite plainly—my dear little Horbrook!

Of other famous stories about bears which appeared before the advent of the teddy bear, I should perhaps mention the delightful tales about Bre'r Bear in the Uncle Remus books written by an American, Joel Chandler Harris, in the closing years of the nineteenth century. In their own way they heralded the birth, a few years later, of the teddy bear who was in effect the descendant of all these bears I have just discussed.

3

THE FATHER OF
THE TEDDY BEAR

The man to whom we owe a debt of gratitude for our little friend the teddy bear was none other than a President of the United States of America, Theodore Roosevelt, who was born in 1858 and died in 1919. He was the twenty-sixth person to hold that great office and, as the many biographies of him have shown, he was a larger-than-life figure much loved by the American people.

Theodore Roosevelt was of rugged Dutch and Scottish ancestry and, although born in New York, he quickly grew to love the great outdoors of America. While still in his teens he became a skilled rider, a crack-shot huntsman and a bold explorer. But his life was dedicated to public service, and in 1884 he became leader of the New York legislature, going on to hold the offices of President of the New York Police Board and Assistant Secretary to the US Navy.

His name came to widespread public attention in 1898 when he raised and commanded a group of men known as 'Roosevelt's Rough Riders' who fought in the Cuban War. This activity enabled him to draw on all the backwoods lore he had learned as a young man and his troops became a fighting force to be reckoned with.

On his return to America Roosevelt was made Governor of New York State, and then in 1901 he became the Republican Vice-President. That same year, following the assassination of the incumbent President, William McKinley, he assumed the highest office in the land.

In the years that followed, when the duties of statesmanship permitted, Roosevelt liked to relax by recapturing the pleasures of his youth, hunting with groups of friends. His great passion was hunting bears, in particular grizzlies or, if they were not to be found, the more common black and brown bears. But the President was not solely interested in killing, as he explained in his book, *Outdoor Pastimes of an American Hunter*, published in 1905:

(Above left) Rare sketches drawn by President Roosevelt for his children, of an amusing incident that occurred during one hunt: 'The Bear Plays Dead' and 'The Bear Sits Up!'

(Above right) Contemporary photograph of President Roosevelt out bear-hunting. (Underwood & Underwood, New York, 1902).

Frequently I have been able to watch bears for some time while myself unobserved. With other game I have very often done this even when within close range, not wishing to kill creatures needlessly, or without a good object; but with bears, my experience has been that chances to secure them come so seldom as to make it very distinctly worth while improving any that do come, and I have not spent much time watching any bear unless he was in a place where I could not get at him, or else was so close at hand that I was not afraid of his getting away.

On one occasion the bear was hard at work digging up squirrel or gopher caches on the side of a pine-clad hill; while at this work he looked rather like a big badger. On two other occasions the bear was fussing around a carcass preparatory to burying it. On these occasions I was very close, and it was extremely interesting to note the grotesque, half-human movements, and giant, awkward strength of the great beast. He would twist the carcass around with the utmost ease, sometimes taking it in his teeth and dragging it, at other times grasping it in his forepaws and half-lifting, half shoving it. Once the bear lost his grip and rolled over during the course of some movement, and this made him angry, and he struck the carcass a savage whack, just as a pettish child will strike a table against which it has knocked itself.

At another time I watched a black bear some distance off getting his breakfast under stumps and stones. He was very active, turning the log or stone over, and then thrusting his muzzle into the empty space to gobble up the small creatures below, before they recovered from their surprise and the sudden inflow of light. From under one log he got a chipmunk, and danced hither and thither with even more agility than awkwardness, slapping at the chipmunk with his paw while it zigzagged about, until finally he scooped it into his mouth.

President Roosevelt found the habits of grizzly bears particularly interesting, he said, and noticed their variations of temper. 'There are savage and cowardly bears', he wrote, 'just as there are big and little ones; and sometimes these variations are very marked among bears of the same district, and at other times all the bears of one district will seem to have a common code of behaviour which differs utterly from that of the bears of another district.'

Although the President was a brave and skilful hunter, he did have one close shave with a bear which he described in his autobiography, written in 1913:

The only narrow escape I met with was from a grizzly bear. It was about 24 years ago. I had wounded the bear just at sunset, in a wood of lodgepole pines, and, following him, I wounded him again, as he stood on the other side of a thicket. He then charged through the

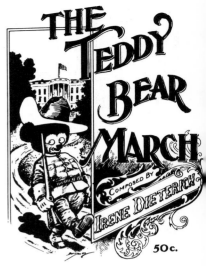

'The Teddy Bear March' by Irene Dietrich was one of many tunes composed about the association of the President with teddy bears. The illustration is by Clifford Berryman.

Cartoon by Clifford Berryman of President Theodore Roosevelt's famous bear hunt in November 1902, which resulted in the birth of the teddy bear.

Roosevelt and his 'Teddy' – a cartoon entitled 'Teddy in Timberland' by C.A. Macauley (1907).

brush, coming with such speed and with such an irregular gait that, try as I would, I was not able to get the sight of my rifle on the brain-pan, though I hit him very hard with both the remaining barrels of my magazine Winchester.

After my last shot, the first thing I saw was the bear's left paw as he struck at me, so close that I made a quick movement to one side. He was, however, practically already dead, and after another jump, and while in the very act of trying to turn to come at me, he collapsed like a shot rabbit.

It was on the afternoon of 14 November, 1902, however, that the incident occurred which gave birth to our little friend, the teddy bear.

President Roosevelt was visiting the South that month. He had made the journey to settle a boundary dispute which had arisen between Mississippi and Louisiana, and planned to draw a new line between the two states to settle the matter. During a break in the negotiations, he was invited to go on a special hunting expedition which had been arranged for him at Smedes on the Mississippi Delta. The organisers of the trip were well-meaning folk and were naturally anxious that their special guest should be assured of shooting at least one bear. When none materialised during the normal course of the hunt, a frantic search was begun to find one.

Unfortunately all the searchers could locate was one small bear cub which they drove towards the position where the President was standing, rifle in hand. The great man took one look at the little creature and turned his back. He drew the line at killing anything so small, he is alleged to have said.

There is, however, another version of this incident. According to Gregory C. Wilson of Massachusetts, a devoted researcher of both Theodore Roosevelt and the teddy bear, the bear which the President refused to shoot was not a cub but a full-grown animal. In an article, 'The Birth of the Teddy Bear', in the Fall 1979 issue of the American *Bear Tracks* magazine, he describes the day of the hunt and the fruitless search for a bear, in particular the efforts of one of the local guides, whom he names as Holt Collier:

By early afternoon T. R. felt Collier must have lost track of the bear so they returned to camp. Soon after they returned, they heard Collier's horn indicating a bear was at bay. They ran to the spot where they found Collier had a huge 230-pound bear entangled with ropes and surrounded by dogs. It was an old bear and lame in one foot. Several people shouted, 'Let the President shoot the

Another satirical cartoon of the President by Jim Flohri for *Judge* magazine, 9 February, 1907.

27

President Roosevelt 'draws the line' at shooting the bear cub – another Clifford Berryman cartoon.

bear', but the embarrassed T. R. would not take a trophy in such an unsportsmanlike manner. Indicating he would not shoot the bear, he insisted they stop tormenting the animal. John Parker (who later became Governor of Louisiana) requested permission to kill the animal with his hunting knife and T. R. agreed. The bear was killed, skinned and packed up for the Smithsonian Museum. On the way back to camp, the three Associated Press newsmen allowed on the hunt wrote stories which were sent across the country.

But to return to the more widely quoted story of the bear cub. According to one later account the cub was found on its own because it had been deserted by its mother. As it is most unusual for a mother bear to leave a cub, it is suggested the little animal may have fallen from a tree or, more likely, that

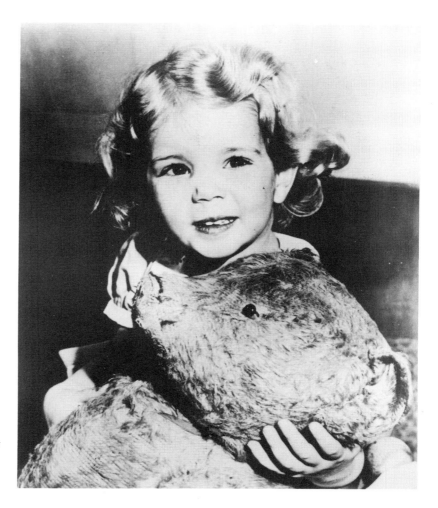

President Roosevelt's great-grandchild, Susan, with the original teddy bear made by Morris Michtom, which helped launch a worldwide phenomenon.

it had fled from a forest fire and thus become separated from its parent. One persistent legend maintains that the cub's fur was actually singed and that this is one of the main reasons why the Department of Agriculture adopted the bear as the symbol for their campaign to try to prevent forest fires and also called the character 'Smokey the Bear'.

In any event, President Roosevelt did not enjoy the encounter and later confided his feelings to a friend, Philip Stewart, in a letter dated 24 November, 1902:

> I have just had a most unsatisfactory experience on a bear hunt in Mississippi. There were plenty of bears, and if I had gone alone or with one companion, I would have gotten one or two. But my kind hosts, with the best of intentions, insisted upon turning the affair into a cross between a hunt and a picnic, which always results in

failure for the hunt and usually in failure for the picnic. On this occasion, as a picnic it was pleasant enough, but as a hunt simply exasperating, and I never got a shot. Naturally the comic press jumped at the failure and have done a good deal of laughing over it!

This might well have been the end of the matter if one of the most famous cartoonists of the day had not heard of the incident and immortalised it in a cartoon. The double meaning of the sketch is underlined by its caption, 'Drawing the line in Mississippi!' The cartoonist's name was Clifford K. Berryman of the *Washington Evening Star* and after its initial appearance on 18 November the drawing was soon being republished all over America.

Clifford Berryman's daughter has added a little more detail to the shooting incident, which she recounted in a letter: 'Every time I heard father tell this story, he concluded by saying that when Roosevelt saw the tiny cub he said, "If I shot that little fellow, I couldn't look my own children in the face".'

Mr Gregory Wilson, in his article 'The Birth of the Teddy Bear', has a slightly different interpretation to put on the double meaning of the cartoon's caption. He says that Berryman's reference to Roosevelt 'drawing the line' was an unsubtle pun on the 'colour line', as the President was then a strong supporter of civil rights for America's black people and was attracting a lot of hostility towards his views in the South. Mr Wilson writes, 'The cartoon clearly showed T. R. would not shoot "black bears" brought to him on ropes. It graphically portrayed T. R.'s unyielding support of black civil rights.' Mr Wilson closes his fascinating but controversial report with the statement, 'Thus, the Teddy Bear was born as a result of a racial pun.'

What remains beyond dispute is that neither the President nor Clifford Berryman could possibly have realised then that they had played such crucial parts in 'creating' the teddy bear.

4

WHO MADE THE FIRST TEDDY BEAR?

One of the most surprising aspects of the story of the teddy bear is that it is almost impossible to say who made the very first one! Indeed, the very first bearlike cuddly toys were created at virtually the same time, quite unbeknown to one another, on the opposite sides of the Atlantic!

If we are being exact about the term 'teddy bear', then the earliest example was certainly made by an American, but there is no disputing that a German manufacturer made a cuddly toy bear at the self-same time. And without wishing to confuse the issue further, it has to be stated that the Russians, with their long tradition of love for the bear, had been making replicas of the creature for centuries, in everything from fur to wood. However, in this book we are primarily concerned with the teddy bear, so let us consider the American and German claims as being of greater importance.

It is perhaps not altogether surprising that it was a Russian immigrant to the United States who made the first teddy bear. The man's name was Morris Michtom and his mind was steeped in the traditions from the old country: he had even had wooden replicas of bears among his childhood toys. He appreciated only too well that the symbolism of the bear was as deeply rooted in the consciousness of the nation as that of the eagle in America and the bulldog in Britain, and knew many of the stories about Russia's most famous bear, Mishka, hero of a hundred folk tales.

At the crucial moment in our story, however, he was running a small stationery and novelty store on Thompson Avenue in the Brooklyn district of New York.

Mr Michtom was a hard-working, intelligent man, always trying to anticipate the new interests among his customers and thereby increase his business. Both he and his wife Rose were clever with their hands, and frequently made dolls and other small playthings to sell alongside the sweets and confectionery. He was well aware that children needed dolls and animal toys to whom they could confide their troubles.

31

Morris Michtom and a model of one of 'Teddy's Bears'.

It was when Morris Michtom saw Clifford Berryman's cartoon of 'Teddy Roosevelt's Bear', in November 1902, that he had the idea which was to make him famous. He decided he would create a toy replica of the delightful little bear which the kind-hearted President could not bring himself to shoot.

Morris mentioned the idea to Rose. She immediately agreed with him, and sat down to plan how to make not one, as legend would have it, but two stuffed bears. In order that they should look authentic, she chose honey-coloured plush for the fur and cut a strip into two bear shapes, carefully making allowance for the creature's familiar 'humped' back. Then she sewed the edges together, filled all the parts with excelsior, and attached the bears' limbs and paws to the body so that they were movable. For the creatures' eyes she picked boot buttons and used stitching thread for their mouths. When complete, the pair of bears stood two-and-a-half feet tall.

The following day Morris Michtom put the bears on display in his shop window, with a notice that the selling price was $1.50 each. Before he closed that night both had been sold, and several disappointed customers had indicated that if Rose would make some more they would be happy to buy them. The toys were still, at this time, unnamed: but an idea was already growing in Morris's head. He would call them 'Teddy's Bears'—but perhaps he should first have the President's permission to market them under that name.

A rare early advertisement by Morris Michtom's Ideal Novelty Company, circa 1907.

Rather nervously, the Brooklyn shopkeeper had his wife make up a special bear and posted it off to the White House with a letter explaining what he had done and asking whether the President would mind his name being used in this context. Mr Michtom waited apprehensively for the reply, sensing that if the answer was no, his good idea would be ruined.

If the answer *had* been no, of course, our little friend the teddy bear might never have come into existence.

When a letter arrived from Washington, Mr Michtom tore open the envelope with shaking hands. Inside was a brief note in the President's own handwriting. The shopkeeper's heart jumped for joy at what he read.

'Dear Mr Michtom', the reply said, 'I don't think my name is likely to be worth much in the toy bear business, but you are welcome to use it.'

So, with the President's approval, Mr Michtom prepared to develop the production of 'Teddy's Bears'. And by the following year he had a team of workers manufacturing them by the hundreds and had established himself as the Ideal Novelty and Toy Company. In 1907 the company became a corporation and went on to be one of the biggest toy manufacturers in America until, in 1982, it was taken over by CBS, Inc., and ceased to produce bears.

Margarete Steiff and one of the many bears which still carry her name.

In 1903 it was impossible to patent a trade name, and it was not long before others were copying Mr Michtom's success. Before the new century was a decade old there were at least a dozen other teddy bear manufacturers in America: one, based in Chicago, was even called the Theodore Bear Company.

When Morris Michtom died in 1938 his family received a letter of condolence from President Roosevelt's widow and newspapers throughout the nation mourned the passing of 'The Teddy Bear Man'.

To tell the story of the other person who began making toy bears at this time we must cross the Atlantic to Germany, another nation with a long tradition of making outstanding children's toys. The central figure in this episode was a remarkable young woman named Margarete Steiff (pronounced Shtyff), the daughter of a master builder, who was born in 1847 at Giengen-an-der-Brenz, Württemberg, in the picturesque Black Forest region.

Unhappily, tragedy struck Margarete when she was only two years old—she contracted polio which left both her legs paralysed and she had to spend the rest of her life in a wheelchair. However, she was not a person to let her infirmity spoil her life or restrict her energetic mind: as she grew to maturity she found she possessed great skill in the parts of her body not affected by the polio, her hands, and she quickly became an accomplished seamstress—she and her sister owned the first hand-driven sewing machine in Giengen. Although she herself never married, Margarete developed a great love for children, and when little friends came to visit her she took to making them small animals out of the remnants of cloth she had left over from dressmaking, her primary vocation. The first of these toy animals, made in 1880, was a felt elephant.

In the beginning she gave the little figures away, but soon more of her acquaintances, both young and old, began wanting the elephants. According to the Steiff family records, Margarete made eight of them in 1880, by 1885 she had made 596, and the following year over 5,000. In 1886 a monkey was added to the line, followed by a donkey, horse, pig and camel. To fulfil the demand, the young seamstress naturally had to take on members of her family as well as local women to help her.

By the close of the century Margarete was producing a whole range of soft toy animals, and then in 1902, her eldest nephew, Richard Steiff, who had been employed to create new lines, brought her another idea. It was a toy bear, with movable head and limbs, a long pointed snout and black boot buttons for eyes, which he had designed as a result of observing brown bears in the Zoological Gardens in Stuttgart

Rare photograph of Margarete Steiff at work in the Giengen-an-der-Brenz factory where the legend began.

while studying for his degree in art. Initially, apparently, she was not taken with the idea, as the bear was made in brown mohair plush which was difficult to obtain and it was larger than traditional toy animals.

The following year, however, at the annual Leipzig Toy Fair, fate intervened on behalf of the bear. A buyer from F. A. O. Schwartz called at the Steiff stand and said he was having no luck in finding something soft and cuddly for the American market. The family tried without success to interest him in their various lines, and had almost given up hope when they remembered the despised fluffy bear.

According to Steiff family legend, the buyer took one look at the little creature and to everyone's surprise promptly placed an order for 3,000 of them!

When the news of the sale was relayed to Margarete Steiff, back in her workshop in the Black Forest, she had to admit she had been wrong not to share Richard's belief in the toy. Nevertheless she quickly generated the enthusiasm to fulfil the order—and within months it was clear that the toy bear was destined to become Steiff's most successful line.

Over the next year twelve thousand of these bears were exported, mostly to America and England. By 1907 there were four hundred factory hands and eighteen hundred women working in their homes to keep pace with the orders pouring into Giengen. (According to Steiff records, in 1907 the output reached 974,000, and although this has subsequently proved to be an all-time peak, in 1953, the golden anniversary of the teddy bear, production was at a steady quarter of a million per year and this figure has remained constant every year since.)

The year 1908 saw the introduction of the 'growler' which caused the teddy bear, when tilted backwards, to make an animal noise in the same way that the 'squeaker' apparatus makes a baby doll cry. Further developments which the Steiffs introduced were bears that could be dressed up and (when the term 'teddy bear' was in common usage) the 'Teddy Bear Baby'. Steiff bears were easily distinguishable from all others by having a small button inserted in their ears—the symbol being referred to as *knopf im ohr*.

It is interesting to note that once the term 'teddy bear' was universally accepted, the word 'Bruin', which had been used by children for centuries when referring to baby bears, disappeared to be replaced by 'Teddy'. Other generally recognised nursery names such as 'Bunny' for rabbit and 'Pussy' for cat have, however, never changed.

Although Margarete Steiff died in May 1909, she had lived long enough to witness the universal acceptance of the teddy bear by both girls and boys, and the company which carries her name still flourishes in Giengen today. In local parlance it is not surprisingly often referred to as the 'Teddy Bear Town'.

With hindsight, it is perhaps fair to say that while it was Morris Michtom who created and named the teddy bear as we know it today, it was Margaret Steiff who popularised it and started the worldwide craze for bears. At all events, it

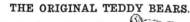

THE ORIGINAL TEDDY BEARS.

Genuine Imported Teddy Bears with voices. Made by Margaret Steiff.

Steiff bears across the years: some of the most popular models made during the firm's first 75 years.

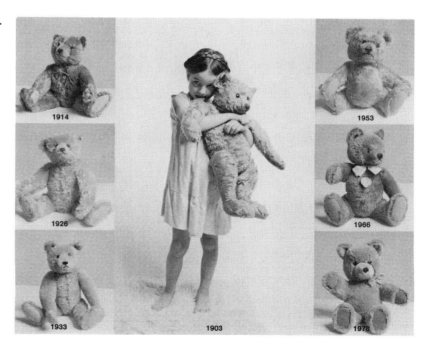

became a phenomenon during both their lifetimes far beyond anything they could have imagined.

But to return to our history. In his book *Children's Toys Throughout the Ages* (1953), Leslie Daiken has some interesting things to tell us about what was happening in Britain during those early days:

> While this toy drama was unfolding in the Black Forest, the idea occurred to British makers that, since the plush used in the German bears came from Yorkshire, it would be feasible to manufacture Teddies in Britain. In order to compete with cheap labour abroad, the shape was modified. The long, thin Teddy was being made on the principle of the German soft dolls of the period, which consisted of a large bag for the body and four long thin sacks for each limb. The English makers radically changed this shape by shortening the body, making the limbs better proportioned and giving a plumper appearance to the animal. The earliest English bears were filled

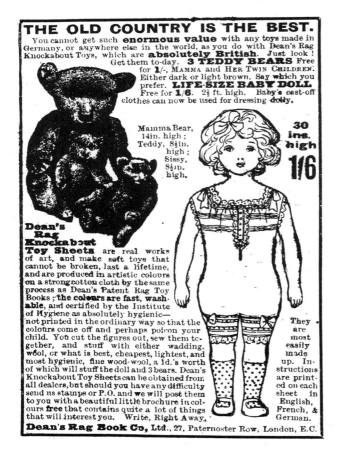

Dean's Rag Book Co. Ltd of London were one of the earliest British manufacturers of teddy bears. This advertisement appeared in *Home Chat*, November 1908.

with kapok, a soft, resilient, natural material grown mostly in Indonesia. The head was enlarged and filled with wood-wool, a type of wood shavings of a finer quality than that used for packing of wooden cases. A new method was perfected for joining the limbs which insured a tight fit to the body. All wires that might injure a young child were left out. This method of fixing is a closely guarded secret among the manufacturers of Teddy Bears to this day. Toys in which growlers are inserted must be hand-filled with wood-wool, as kapok, being soft and fluffy, would enter the holes of the voice-box, and prevent the growl from functioning.

The speed with which the world's children took to the teddy bear was nothing short of amazing, and soon the little creatures were making friends all round the globe—and of all ages, too. It has been argued in some quarters that the reason for the teddy bear's success was that it came onto the market at a time when there was a great need for a toy for boys, dolls being considered unsuitable for them. Just as dolls appealed to the feminine and maternal instincts in girls, so the toy bears appealed to the masculine, hunting and parental instincts in boys. What really happened, of course, was that both sexes found the little creatures absolutely irresistible!

Association with the President was also used by other teddy bear makers as this 1910 advertisement reveals.

39

President Roosevelt himself could hardly fail to be aware of this furore, and when he campaigned again for the Presidency in 1904 he adopted a bear as his campaign symbol. Manufacturers responded to this by turning out commemorative plates featuring the President and his namesake, as well as stick pins, blazer buttons and scarves. A composer named William R. Haskins wrote what proved to be the first of over 400 songs to feature teds, 'Teddy's Bears', and alongside the ranges of bears to be found in shops and stores there appeared new variations of old games such as 'Feed the Bear' (based on the game of pinning a tail on a donkey while blindfold) and jigsaws like 'Teddy and his Bear'.

Clifford K. Berryman watched with a mixture of amazement and amusement as the toys inspired by his cartoon swept the nation, but not once did he express a regret that he had not copyrighted the idea and reaped a flood of royalties. 'I have made thousands of children happy,' he was quoted as saying in a rare interview, 'and that is enough for me.' He did, however, retain the figure of the little bear as a kind of personal trademark and for years afterwards the 'original' teddy was to be found gambolling somewhere in all his cartoons. Berryman's skill as a political cartoonist was finally recognised in 1944 when he was awarded a Pulitzer Prize.

It was in 1906 that the 'Teddy Bear Craze' really took a grip of America, as the newspapers and magazines of the period reveal. From all over the country came reports of stores struggling in vain to keep pace with demand—a precursor of the present-day rush every Christmas for the 'must-have' toy of the moment—and in the weekly and monthly journals advertisements placed by the major stores competed with one another to offer the latest teddy bears. The magazine *Playthings* devoted almost an entire issue to what it called

The Teddy Bear Craze: four examples from American magazines of 1907.

THE LATEST TEDDY BEAR NOVELTY
The name and design will d the work.
F 1369 — Teddy Bea Stationery. The ever popula subject in a new idea, this bo is beautifully lithographed an does full justice to the "Tedd Bear" idea; the paper is th finest quality of cloth finis stock with wallet velopes
Per doz 1.8

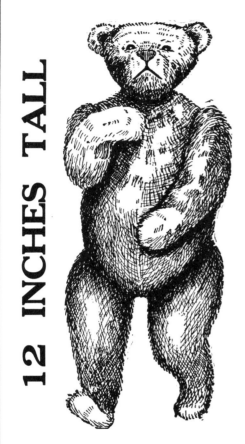

'The Plush Bear Craze' and informed its readers somewhat breathlessly:

> Never in our history has the country been more at the mercy of bears than it is today. Stuffed plush teddies are fairly rampant, and indications show prospects of a long and continued reign for Majesty Bruin. Department stores are stocking up with them for a while, but not for long, because as soon as the youthful hunters get on their tracks, they swoop down and bring them to bay. One New York store, the largest we have, has already sold over sixty thousand teddies, and every week it gets hundreds of dozens which are bought up at once.

The craze soon reached such a pitch that doll manufacturers began to fear their sales would be adversely affected, and it required a leader in *Playthings* to allay their worries. 'A Teddy Bear', the Editor wrote, 'is a toy, and a doll is a doll, and every little girl wants a doll, and the fact that she wants a bear will not diminish that desire.'

In another fascinating article, 'Teddy's Bear', in the American antiques magazine *Spinning Wheel* (April 1971), Emma Stiles says of the Teddy Bear Craze at this time:

> The Teddy Bears were not only a toy for youngsters, aged one to ten. They became collectors' items for teenagers of both sexes who lavished as much affection on them as the little tots did. The unparalleled furore of Teddy Bears worried a number of people. Editorials began to appear in journals scorning women who carried Teddy Bears about with them. A Michigan priest denounced the Teddy Bear as 'destroying all instincts of motherhood and leading to race suicide'. Within four years of Teddy's introduction to the toy world, almost every child had one.

Miss Stiles notes that the craze became so widespread that manufacturers were making every conceivable kind of toy carrying the teddy bear name:

> There were Teddy Bear pails, tea sets, carts and cages; there were puzzles and games. Teddy Bear stationery came on the market. There were Teddy Bear muzzles, leashes, squeeze balls, hammocks, postcards, candy boxes, favors, party games, balloons, shooflies, rocking horses, books, card games, pins, rubber stamps, water pistols, scarfs, banks, blocks, wagons, targets and paper dolls, even Teddy Bear briefcases made of plush. Pedal

cars were advertised with bears driving them. Strauss, the toy king, made a self-whistling Teddy Bear. There were boats made to fit any bear. A tumbling bear was made, and a bear with a doll's face. The craze kept on and on. Teddy Bears were everywhere ...

Unlike many crazes, however, this one did not die out when President Roosevelt left office. Many of the spin-offs certainly disappeared, but the demand for teddies themselves remained constant. Those that got lost were quickly replaced, and any that were almost loved to death were carefully repaired. Durability became the bear's middle name.

A story is told of Roosevelt's trip to Cambridge University during his visit to England in 1905. There a group of students dangled a teddy bear on a piece of string from an upper window just as he was passing by. Without the slightest show of embarrassment the great man halted, took hold of his namesake and solemnly shook his hand! In America he doubtless heard the most popular of corny jokes about him: 'If Theodore is President of America with his clothes on, what is he with them off?'—'Teddy Bare!'

One can only wonder today what the reaction of this remarkable man might be to the fact that his most enduring fame is not as a statesman, or as a reformer, or even as a hunter, but for giving his name to perhaps the most popular and beloved of all cuddly toys.

It has also been suggested that the teddy bear got its name from King Edward VII who, when Prince of Wales, visited the London Zoo in 1880 and took a particular fancy to a small Australian koala bear which had recently arrived. However, although the koala is known in Australia as the teddy bear, there is no evidence to suggest that this visit gave rise to the term—all the more so because the koala is quite different in appearance from the first toy bears that were made.

President Roosevelt's encounter with the bear cub takes on almost mythic status in Sarah Noble Ives' retelling of the legend published at the height of the 'Teddy Bear Craze' in 1907.

The Juvenile Book of the Season

THE WONDERFUL STORY OF TEDDY THE BEAR

Written and Illustrated in Colors
BY SARAH NOBLE IVES

Large Quarto, Lithographic Covers,
PRICE, $0.75

A beautiful story told for our young people, and containing a wholesome lesson.

McLoughlin Bros., 890 Broadway, New York

5

THE ADVENTURES OF THE ROOSEVELT BEARS

Although the teddy bear craze created a public demand for all manner of related items, books about the new character were slower to appear. Those that came onto the market, however, were in time to become valuable and eagerly sought after by collectors. Of these the most popular and now most coveted were the adventures of two characters known as Teddy-B and Teddy-G, 'The Roosevelt Bears', created by Seymour Eaton.

These two high-spirited and ingenious bears admittedly looked rather more like real bears than teddies, but the source of their inspiration was obvious and they found immediate acceptance among readers when their adventures, in pictures and rhyming verse, began to appear in newspapers across America. From 1905 onwards, young and old alike waited impatiently for each day's newspaper to follow the latest rollicking episode about the two bears. For a year the adventures were syndicated through twenty newspapers, and then the first of four books compiled from the serial appeared.

The first title in the series was *The Roosevelt Bears—Their Travels and Adventures* (1906) which ran to 180 pages with both black and white and coloured illustrations by V. Floyd Campbell. The lively verses accompanying the pictures described the bears' experiences as they travelled by train from their home in the Rocky Mountains to New York. The second book, *More About the Roosevelt Bears* (1906) continued the bears' adventures in New York and described their return journey to Colorado, including a meeting with their namesake on the way! The illustrations in this volume were by R. K. Culver and followed the style established by Floyd Campbell.

The third book, arguably the best, was *The Roosevelt Bears Abroad* (1907) and was again illustrated by R. K. Culver. This took the bears across the Atlantic to Britain (where they met

Seymour Eaton's Roosevelt Bears were very popular characters during the 'Teddy Bear Craze' in America.

King Edward), through Europe and then home by way of Egypt. The final book in the series was *The Bear Detectives* (1908) in which Seymour Eaton described how Teddy-B and Teddy-G solved several mysteries concerning a number of nursery characters, including the whereabouts of the tails belonging to Little Bo-Peep's sheep! The illustrations for this volume were by Francis P. Wightman and William K. Sweeney.

Collectors of these books have sometimes been surprised to come across smaller volumes of adventures of the two bears. These editions had fewer coloured plates and sold for 40 cents instead of the $1.50 asked for the first four titles. The books were in fact published about the time of the First World War and were actually episodes taken from the original four volumes—hence their titles which included *The Adventures of the Travelling Bears, The Travelling Bears in New York, The Travelling Bears in Out-Door Sports, The Travelling Bears Across the Sea, The Travelling Bears in England,* and so on. Though easier to find than the original four, these reprint volumes are nonetheless eagerly sought after and fetch quite high prices.

In an article, 'Teddy Bear Fever', in *Spinning Wheel* (June 1972), Julie and Linda Masterson have written:

> In popularity, teddy bear stories were only second to the teddy bear itself, and none were in greater demand than those written by Seymour Eaton. However, this admiration for Teddy-B and Teddy-G was not shared by everyone. Some educators and librarians felt the stories lacked literary merit, but then Seymour Eaton never claimed any for his stories. He repeatedly stated, 'The story is simply a good, wholesome yarn, arranged in a merry jingle and fitted to the love of incident and adventure which is evident in every healthy child.'

Seymour Eaton said that he based a few of his stories on acts of mischief committed by children he knew, and this may well have caused a number of libraries to refuse to stock his titles—a fate also suffered by another contemporary writer later to enjoy worldwide fame, L. Frank Baum, author of *The Wizard of Oz*. Despite Eaton's undoubted popularity, no place has been found for him in any of the standard reference books on children's writers of this period.

However, I have been fortunate in making contact with the author's youngest daughter, Jean Eaton Warren, of Larchmont in New York, who has filled in some of the details about her father.

'I've always been proud of him,' she told me. 'Dad was both creative and promotive. I was only ten when he died

The Roosevelt Bears meet Edward VII who is also associated with the teddy bear story and credited in some quarters with inspiring the first teddies. Illustration from *The Travelling Bears* by R.K. Culver.

suddenly, so I didn't have him for long. He would enter my world of pretend, or take me as a "young lady" to dinner and the theatre. But best of all were the bedtime stories. I'd pick a subject and he would just weave a story about it.'

Like the Roosevelt bears with their wanderlust, Seymour Eaton spent much of his life moving from place to place. He was born on a farm in Ontario, Canada, to parents who had emigrated from Ireland. After schooling, he took up a post in education and in his early twenties became principal of a high school in Bracebridge, Ontario, where his wife-to-be was a senior. Several years later the couple were married.

After further jobs in Canada, Seymour Eaton moved to Boston and there established America's first correspondence school. Ten years later the family moved again—to Philadelphia, where Seymour combined the job of business administrator at Drexel College with running a pioneer lending library. In 1906 he moved to New York and there began to write the first of the Roosevelt Bears stories while becoming closely involved in the newspaper business. For a number of years he was an advertisement adviser to the *New York Times*, *Vogue* and *Vanity Fair* and, according to his daughter, played an important role in the introduction of colour into press advertising.

'He was very proud of his Irish heritage,' says Mrs Warren. 'Dad spent a lot of time in England, too, and was a member of one of the most elite advertising clubs. He was associated with *The Times* for a while and became very friendly with Lord Northcliffe. I remember he was also a great admirer of Teddy Roosevelt and we have a letter from his son thanking Dad for his books which he and his boys knew all about.

'My whole family is proud of the Roosevelt Bears stories. In fact, it seems I've lived my whole life with teddy bears and I still have one of the original bears in my home. I also recall an air raid alarm during World War II—which turned out to be false—when my daughter put on her coat, got her teddy bear, and said ''I'm ready!'' She just loved her teddy bears until they wore out and I think she even considered taking one with her on her honeymoon!'

Two more of R.K. Culver's distinctive illustrations of Teddy-B and Teddy-G during their travels in Ireland and Scotland.

After Seymour Eaton's death the popularity of the two bears declined. Then, in 1945, an article about teddy bears in *Life* magazine prompted many letters from readers, and Mrs Warren and the other members of the family tried to get the original books republished. I am happy to report that the first title in the series, *The Roosevelt Bears—Their Travels and Adventures*, has now been reissued in paperback and there are plans for the others, too.

One of the mysteries that has persisted about Teddy-B and Teddy-G to this day is what their initials stand for. It has been suggested that they are Teddy-Bad and Teddy-Good, although the respective bears do not show such characteristics exclusively. For a time it was thought that the letters were used to distinguish between bears designated as boys or girls, because of the highly advertised line of 'Teddy Boy and Teddy Girl Clothes' made by the firm of Kahn & Mossbacher at the time of the great teddy bear 'fad'. In fact the answer is much simpler than this, and is to be found on page eleven of *The Travelling Bears*, today the hardest of all the Seymour Eaton titles to find. The significant lines read:

> The black bear's name was Teddy-B;
> The B for black or brown, you see.
> And Teddy-G was the gray bear's name;
> The G for gray; but both bears came
> For 'Teddy' because everywhere
> Children called them Teddy Bears.
>
> The 'Teddy' part is a name they found
> On hat and tree and leggins round,
> On belt and boot and plates of tin,
> And scraps of paper and biscuits thin,
> And other things a hunter dropped
> At a mountain camp where he had stopped.
>
> And how some boys, the stories tell
> Liked these two Teddy Bears so well
> That they made a million for the stores to sell;
> Some quite little, for children small,
> And some as big as the bears are tall;
> The brown ones looking like Teddy-B.
> And the white as funny as Teddy-G.

Although it is possible that some copies of the Roosevelt Bears' books found their way across the Atlantic, it was not until 1909 that the first British book to feature a teddy bear appeared. Entitled *The Tale of Teddy Bright-Eyes*, it is the story of a naughty little boy who is punished by being turned into a living teddy bear by 'The Bad Boys' Fairy', Lady Thingummyjig. The book describes his adventures trying to get turned back into his former self.

No author is credited on the cover or title page of this undoubtedly important work, and all attempts to discover his or her identity have failed. Copies of the book are also of the utmost rarity, and the example quoted from below was kindly loaned from the collection of Mrs Nita Rigden of Canterbury. The book was published by Humphrey Milford of London and printed by Thomas Forman & Sons of Nottingham, but the records of neither firm can throw any light on the author. The volume measures 77 mm wide by 101 mm deep (3 × 4 ins), has a four-colour cover but is without illustrations inside. The anonymous author's style is rather reminiscent of blank verse, as this opening episode will demonstrate:

THE TALE OF TEDDY BRIGHTEYES

There was once a very naughty boy, he was round and fat and stumpy, the sort that ought to be merry and gay; but he was sulky and grumpy. He was always saying 'Shan't' and 'Won't!' and 'Do as I like' and 'Don't care', as cross as two sticks. And every one called him a Regular Little Bear.

One day he'd been especially bad. He'd been put in the corner once for doing his lessons so badly (he was really a perfect dunce, for he wouldn't take the trouble to learn). He'd been put in the corner twice, for quarrelling with his sisters, to whom he was never nice; so at last his mother sent him out-of-doors in sheer despair; and he spent his time in trying to find how best to be naughty there.

Teddy, for that was his name, to begin with, swung with all his force on the garden gate. This was forbidden—that's why he did it, of course. And as the hinges creaked and squeaked, and bang, bang, bang went the gate, he saw a little old woman coming; she walked at a wonderful rate for one so old. And she said to him, politely, 'I beg your pardon, but could you tell me whereabouts is the Little Wee Bear Garden?'

Teddy had not the least idea what she was talking about. He turned his back on her, slammed the gate, and rudely replied, 'Find out!'

Then the old woman grew and grew, and rose up tall and big, and said 'I'm the Bad Boys' Fairy, the Lady Thingummyjig. I've heard you were a regular Bear—I've come for myself to see. And, Master Teddy, a Bear you are, and a Bear you shall henceforth be, till you find the Little Wee Bear Garden, and that you won't do just yet, I promise you, you shall be very sorry that ever you

The Tale of Teddy Brighteyes

The first English book about a teddy bear, *The Tale of Teddy Brighteyes*, was published anonymously in 1909.

met with me today. But you've got one chance. If ever you really need help at once—if ever you feel you're very repentant indeed for all your horrid crossness—break off a hawthorn twig and call aloud, "Come, B.B.F.! Come, Lady Thingummyjig".' And the tall old woman disappeared.

Well, Teddy, as you may suppose, was all in a tremble and twitter, down from his head to his toes. 'What could she mean?' he said at first: and then, 'It can't be true! I shall not turn to a Teddy Bear! Of course not; people never do.'

But as he spoke, he felt uncomfortable because he saw his hands, before his eyes, were changing into paws! He felt his face in alarm and haste—it was covered with furry hair! 'My goodness me!' said Teddy. 'I *have* turned into a Teddy Bear!'

He ran indoors to his mother—you know, it's the only place is a mother's knee, whenever one's in trouble or disgrace—and she shrieked with fear when she saw him. 'Oh, mother dear!' he exclaimed, 'a terrible thing has happened—I do feel so ashamed.'

And he told her all about it: and then he asked, 'Is it true? Do I really look like a regular Little Bear to you?' His mother was too upset to speak—but she took him by the paw and led him to the looking-glass, and there indeed he saw a regular Little Teddy Bear. And there indeed his last hope ended. The worst of it was, he couldn't see how matters could be mended. As for his mother, she loved him, in spite of the trouble and care he had brought upon her. She cried, and kissed her unfortunate Little Bear.

Of course, the plight of the Little-Boy-Teddy-Bear soon attracts sightseers who begin to hang around the house, and also newspaper photographers anxious to try to take a picture of him. In despair he runs away to try to find the Wee Bear Garden. During his journey he falls asleep and a little girl drags him home thinking he is a giant-sized Teddy Bear! The girl's father turns out to be a doctor and gives the boy some help before he continues on his way. At the climax of the story, Teddy is captured by two men who make him perform as a dancing bear, and in his fright he finally calls for Lady Thingummyjig, promising that he will never again misbehave. The tale ends:

Then Lady Thingummyjig stooped down, and to his immense surprise, she kissed him, with a lovely smile, and beautiful shining eyes. And she said, 'Look round about you!' and behold! he instantly found he was standing under a notice that said, 'The Wee Bear Garden Ground'. Scores and scores of good little Teddy Bears were scampering to and fro—there were swings and ponds with model yachts, and wonderful flowers a-blow, and hoops, and cricket, and skipping-ropes, and everything you can need to make you very happy and very contented indeed. 'You see what a jolly place it is!' said she, 'all full of joy; now, will you stay as a little Bear, or go home as a little boy?' 'Oh, please, go home!' said Teddy. Then she replied, 'I'll take you there straight away!'

He found himself in the Fairy's arms, at home, inside the gate. She kissed him on the eyes and chin, and said,

'When you grow big, tell the other boys and girls about the Lady Thingummyjig. You shan't be called a Bear again, for that would be a shame. For the future, Teddy Bright-Eyes shall be your nice little name. For happy hearts make sparkling eyes, and you shall be happy now! Goodbye, my dear!' and she vanished.

I hardly need to tell you how rejoiced the mother of Teddy was, when she saw this wonderful change that had come upon him. As everything was so exceedingly strange, she said, 'It's no good wondering why things have happened like this. I've got you back, my darling!' and she gave him a hug and a kiss. 'Mother, as long as I'm with you again,' said Teddy, 'that's all *I* care.

'And never, never again, shall I be a regular Little Teddy Bear!'

Another story, delivering much the same moral lesson and in a similar format as *The Tale of Teddy Bright-Eyes*, appeared a year later, but featured a bear rather than a teddy bear. This was *A Bad Little Bear* and again no author was mentioned, although the illustrations are credited to E. Aris and the publishers are given as Henry Frowde. The book tells the story of a naughty little bear who steals a honeycomb and is punished by the bees.

Tim Tubby Toes, which followed four years later in 1914, featured a character who was also passionately fond of honey, but when he stole several jars and ate them all he felt so sick he had to be given a large spoonful of castor oil and packed off to bed! The story was told by Harry Golding with illustrations by M. M. Rudge. The book was one of a series of 'Little Wonder Books' published by Ward, Lock & Co Ltd just prior to the First World War.

The format of *Tim Tubby Toes* was identical to that of the Beatrix Potter books published by Frederick Warne of London, and Warne's also introduced a bear at this period who delighted younger readers. *Mrs Bear* was one of the characters who appeared in a series of 'Mr' and 'Mrs' books (not to be confused with the modern 'Mr Men' books by Roger Hargreaves), all of which were illustrated by the talented Lawson Wood whose work is now much coveted by collectors. So popular did Mrs Bear become that she was even featured in advertising for Iron Jelloids tonic pills!

Although there were certainly other books around at this time which featured bears, the important teddy bear characters did not begin to emerge until after the end of the First World War, and such is their importance that they merit separate entries in the next chapter.

6

AN A–Z OF CELEBEARITIES

ALBERT
(Great Britain, b. 1968)
In the Seventies, Albert, the little Cockney bear from London's East End, became a tremendous children's favourite. His creator, Alison Jezard, originally wanted to write some stories about a kind of Winnie-the-Pooh figure brought up to date and getting involved in adventures in contemporary situations—in fact she has created a unique character who has become instantly recognisable in his cloth cap, due in large measure to Margaret Gordon's excellent pictures. Albert is a very friendly bear who lives at the delightful address of 14 Spoonbasher's Row, not far from his great friend, Henry the junk-cart horse. His other particular pals who feature in his adventures are his cousin Angus from Scotland, Tum-Tum the Panda, and the robust Digger the koala.

ANDY PANDY'S TEDDY
(Great Britain, b. 1951)
Andy Pandy's Teddy was the first teddy bear to become a television star. Andy himself is a little clown, but a clever one, and it is poor Teddy who invariably gets into trouble or does something silly. Andy Pandy first appeared on British television in the programme 'Watch with Mother' in 1950, but it was not until the following year that Teddy made his bow. The films featuring Andy, Teddy and their other friend, Looby Loo, a rag doll, have been widely shown abroad (particularly in Australia and New Zealand) and more recently stories about the trio have been appearing in children's comics.

BIG TEDDY AND LITTLE TEDDY
(Great Britain, b. 1916)
Big Teddy and Little Teddy were an inseparable pair who appeared in stories written by Mrs H. C. Craddock in the years between the two World Wars and were as popular with

young readers then as Paddington and Rupert are today. The large, gruff Big Teddy with his little friend who was missing an arm and a leg were two of the toys belonging to a small girl called Josephine and they, perhaps more than any of the others, were the cause of any mischief or naughtiness that occurred in the stories. Mrs Craddock is believed to have based her books on the toys and teddy bears owned by her own daughter, Margaret, and no doubt their popularity was helped considerably by the many attractive and colourful illustrations by Honor C. Appleton which appeared in the twelve Josephine books. Little Teddy also has the distinction of being the only important teddy bear character in literature to have some of his limbs missing!

BILLY BLUEGUM
(Australia, b. 1904)

Billy Bluegum, an irascible and highly amusing koala bear, is by far the most famous and popular cartoon animal in Australian history. Ever since the brilliant Norman Lindsay first featured him in a sketch in the Sydney weekly publication, *The Bulletin*, in August 1904, he has risen to become a national hero. (As a matter of interest, Billy did not actually receive his name in Lindsay's illustrations until January 1908.) Billy's adventures, which mirrored Australia's own social developments during the first half of the twentieth century, also appeared in *The Lone Hand*, a monthly magazine published by the same company as *The Bulletin*, and on occasions Norman Lindsay used him in political drawings and allowed him to be in advertising campaigns. Although Lindsay died in 1969, his work has now become highly valued among collectors, and new generations of Australians are enjoying Billy Bluegum through republication of some of his adventures in book form.

BIMBO
(Spain, b. 1965)

Spain's favourite teddy bear is to be found in shops and supermarkets from one end of the country to the other. He's a delightful little chap who is featured on a whole range of bread and cakes, and he and the products carrying his name have been popular with the Spanish people as well as tourists for a good many years now. Anyone who has tasted his wares will agree he's a dab hand at baking!

BUSSI BÄR
(Germany, b. 1969)

Bussi Bär has become firmly established as the favourite teddy bear with German children and his magazine is one of the

best-selling juvenile publications in the country. Bussi, with his captivating, wide-eyed expression, and his faithful friend Bello, a little blue dog, enjoy all manner of exciting adventures which are retold and drawn by their creator, the talented cartoonist Rolf Kauka. 'The Friends of Bussi Bär', as his readers are known, run into many thousands.

CORDUROY
(United States, b. 1968)

The smart little bear Corduroy has found himself a place in the hearts of many American children and has recently crossed the Atlantic to earn the same kind of affection in Britain. Don Freeman, Corduroy's creator, retells his adventures with great charm, from the moment a little black girl's mother refuses to buy him because he is missing a button on one of the straps of his overalls. Naturally upset, Corduroy sets out to find another button, having to overcome a number of dangers in the huge department store where he lives, but although he has no luck, the little girl unexpectedly returns the following day to buy him after all!

THE GRETZ TEDDY BEARS
(United States, b. 1968)

The five teddy bears created by Susanna Gretz are almost child-like in their characteristics, and they all live together in a modern house with a large Dalmatian dog called Fred. The bears, named William, Andrew, Charles, Robert and John, are each a different colour and vary in temperament from William, who is always dreaming of his next meal, to Charles the scholar who is invariably deep in a book. Apart from her own books, Susanna Gretz also illustrates the series of stories about a little bear called Rug, which are written by Helen Cresswell.

GROS NOUNOURS
(France, b. 1962)

Gros Nounours is a French teddy bearlike character who sprang to fame at much the same time as Sooty in Great Britain and the American cartoon bear, Yogi. In fact, bears are not often found in French literature; a short story by Alexandre Dumas, 'Tom: An Adventure of a Bear in Paris', published in the nineteenth century, was one of the few before the sudden and unexpected popularity of Gros Nounours in the 1960s. He is ostensibly a bear, but also has the power to fly when he finds himself in difficult situations! Gros Nounours, who is a great storyteller, began his adventures in a syndicated newspaper series, but found lasting fame when these were turned into a television series which ran for more than 1,000 episodes. Interestingly, French children prefer to call teddy bears 'Martin' rather than the traditional 'Teddy'.

MARY PLAIN
(Great Britain, b. 1930)

Mary Plain is a delightful and mischievous little bear whose first adventure, *Mostly Mary*, appeared in 1930. Of the thirteen subsequent books written by the author Gwynedd Rae, it is pleasing to note that several are still available. Miss Rae got her idea for Mary Plain while visiting the famous Bear Pits in Berne, Switzerland, and indeed the first book, *Mostly Mary*, is made up of incidents she actually observed there. In the stories which followed, Mary showed herself to be something of a character, as capable of getting into trouble as of pulling off some splendid act of rescue, being very brave into the bargain. As well as solving problems and mysteries, she lent a hand in the war effort (*Mary Plain in Wartime*, 1942), travelled

56

extensively (*Mary Plain Goes to America*, 1957, perhaps the best of the books) and earned her place as a literary celebrity (*Mary V.I.P.*, 1961). All her adventures have been illustrated by Irene Williamson.

MISHKA
(Russia, b. circa twelfth century)
The bear has been a favourite in Russian folklore and legends for many centuries and his most common name is Mishka. Performing bears are also a staple in Russian circuses, and for years the most popular sweet with the country's children was a 'Mishka'. Over the years Mishka has been depicted by a whole host of talented artists and it is only possible to mention a couple here. A teddy bear called Mishka is the subject of a cartoon series, and in recent years his adventures have taken him into space as a cosmonaut, emulating the achievements of the Russian spacemen! A rather striking Mishka was also designed by the Russians to serve as the mascot for the Olympic Games held in Moscow in 1980.

MR BEAR

(Japan, b. 1968)

Mr Bear is Japan's favourite bear and his adventures, related by Chizuko Kuratomi, have been delighting Japanese children for a quarter of a century. Recently the stories, complete with Kozo Kakimoto's highly individual illustrations, have been translated into English and gained a strong following among British and American children. Mr Bear lives in Rabbit Town, but his size dwarfs most of the other inhabitants and he has a knack of getting into trouble, however well-meaning his intentions are. Teddy bears are becoming increasingly popular in Japan, with rare examples from America and Europe eagerly sought after by collectors.

ODD

(Great Britain, b. 1971)

The adventures of the little teddy bear Odd, told in seven books by James Roose-Evans, concern his search for the Great Bear. According to legend this Great Bear was present at the Court of King Arthur and has been sleeping in Bear Mountain somewhere in Wales ever since the great king died. The legend says the Great Bear will be woken by another bear to whom he will reveal the whereabouts of the Lost Treasure of Wales. Odd comes to believe he may be this bear and sets off on his exciting and fascinating quest, accompanied by his friend Elsewhere, a circus clown. James Roose-Evans, the author of this imaginative saga, was a teacher, actor and writer, and based the stories on a little teddy bear and a toy clown in his possession.

PADDINGTON

(Great Britain, b. 1956)

Paddington, perhaps more than any other bear in this A–Z, enjoyed an absolutely meteoric rise to fame—his adventures have been translated into more than 22 languages and he appears on television not only in Britain and America, but in France, Germany, Holland, Greece and down under in Australia and New Zealand. He is even featured on a credit card issued by the Mitsui Bank. According to the books by Michael Bond, Paddington was found sitting on Paddington Station in London (hence his name) after a journey from Darkest Peru and with a label attached to him reading, 'Please Look After This Bear. Thank You.' Actually Mr Bond got the idea for him on Christmas Eve 1956 when he was trying to find some last-minute Christmas presents in Selfridge's store in London. He saw a teddy bear sitting all by itself on a shelf. 'I thought the bear looked so lonely that I bought him as a Christmas present for my wife,' says Mr Bond. Ten days later

the new arrival had inspired him to write a story—but it still took two years and five publishers before anyone saw the potential in Paddington. 'He's not a cuddly bear,' Mr Bond says of his creation who he thinks has some of his own characteristics (in particular a love of marmalade and old duffle coats). 'He's a bear for standing up in the corner. That's why he wears wellington boots.'

Paddington has now been the subject of sixteen books and in 1998 celebrates his fortieth anniversary—though he still remains resolutely nine years old, says Mr Bond. Few other types of teddy bear sell over 100,000 models of themselves each year. Although Paddington has been drawn by innumerable artists—among them Fred Banberry, David McKee and Barry Macey—for the enormous range of merchandise (from slippers to wallpaper) on which he appears, the first and original drawings of him by Peggy Fortnum remain the favourites with his admirers. A figure of the little bear from Peru stands on the concourse of the station that gave him his name. Recently, a limited edition of 5,000 Paddington Bears has been produced by Teddy Bears of Witney, in mohair with jointed legs, a leather suitcase, marmalade sandwich and a certificate signed by Michael Bond. And in June 1997 an original Paddington made for the BBC TV series in 1979—one of only two—was offered for auction at Sotheby's with an estimate of £6,000–£10,000. Happily, however, bear awareness triumphed and the owner withdrew him at the last minute.

Photo: *The Independent*/Philip Meech.

RUPERT
(Great Britain, b. 1920)

Rupert Bear is arguably one of the most famous cartoon bears in the world and his adventures have been appearing in the British *Daily Express* since 1920 and have also been published in at least 18 other languages. The stories of the little bear and his friends from the village of Nutwood were first created by Mary Tourtel, the wife of the *Express*'s night editor. Rupert's initial purpose was to be a rival to the *Daily Mail*'s then popular cartoon character, 'Teddy Tail', who had been delighting children since 1915. Mary, an accomplished sketch artist, was also something of a larger-than-life character, having been an aviator and adventurer, breaking air speed records prior to the famous Amy Johnson. She had already published several children's books featuring comic animals and verse, and decided to employ a similar style for her new character designated 'Little Lost Bear'. Following his first appearance in the *Express* on 8 November, 1920, Rupert was soon joined by his friends, Bill Badger, Algy, Edward Trunk, Podgy Pig and the Wise Old Goat—who at one time was the most popular character in the strip! In a short space of time Rupert had become a national favourite with his own fan club, 'The Rupert League', and in their bibliography of him, *The Rupert Index* (1979), W. O. G. Lofts and Derek J. Adley have with some justification called him 'The Mickey Mouse of Great Britain'.

The Rupert success story continued to grow until 1935, when Mary Tourtel was struck with failing eyesight and had to retire. It proved no easy task to find a replacement because of the difficulty of drawing Rupert precisely, and only after an extensive search was Alfred Bestall found. The son of a minister of the Church, Bestall was already providing work for a variety of adult and juvenile publications, and proved an ideal replacement—he continued the strip for the next thirty years until 1965, since when the adventures have been in the hands of a team of artists. The popularity of the little bear has led to his use on all manner of products, including children's clothing, furnishings, tableware, toys, jewellery, confectionery and the like—probably only Paddington has endorsed more items! Like Paddington, Rupert has had his own television series, and the little bear was also a star of the stage and is now destined to feature in a full-length £30 million cartoon film. Lofts and Adley believe that nearly 150 million Rupert books of all descriptions have been sold in the three-quarters of a century since he was created.

SHOE SHOP BEARS
(Great Britain, b. 1962)
The Shoe Shop Bears are a little band of bears who began life in a shoe shop where they were 'adopted' by the shop assistant, Polly. In fact their creator, Margaret J. Baker, got the idea for the stories in January 1962 when she was in a shoe shop in Taunton, Somerset. There she saw three teddies being used to amuse young customers while they were fitted with shoes, and soon ideas for a series of adventures began to emerge in her mind. Since Mrs Baker's first book, *The Shoe Shop Bears* (1964), the original trio of fatherly old Threadbare Boots, motherly Slippers and mischievous little Socks have been joined by Hi-Jinks, a modern nylon bear, and Teabag, a small plastic bear, as well as Hannibal, a toy elephant rescued from a rubbish dump and Banger, a basset hound. The illustrations for the early books in the series were done by the splendid C. Walter Hodges, who was followed by Daphne Rowles and most recently Leslie Wood.

SMOKEY BEAR
(United States, b. 1944)
Smokey is perhaps the best known bear in America with his message about the dangers of forest fires. First introduced on a poster in 1944 by the Department of Agriculture who were trying to find a way of combating a spate of devastating forest fires, Smokey was drawn by the *Saturday Evening Post* illustrator, Albert Staehle—who showed him putting out a fire with a bucket of water—while his name was 'borrowed'

from the legendary New York City fireman, Smokey Joe Martin. The hulking brown bear's message was straight and to the point: 'Smokey says: Care will prevent nine out of ten fires.' Initially he was shown unclothed, but Smokey's almost instantaneous popularity, especially among children, caused a hasty revision of this to show him in the now-familiar ranger hat and pair of denim jeans. In 1953 the Ideal Toy Company became the first of several teddy bear manufacturers to be licensed to produce models of the bear—some of which 'talked' to emphasise the message about fire—and the sales of this bear, with its vinyl head and paws, opened the floodgates to a wide range of collectables including books, posters, mugs, binoculars, money-boxes, clocks and even items of clothing, all of which helped to raise funds for the battle against forest fires. The early models by Ideal, Knickerbocker Toy Co and Dakin are now much sought-after. Young enthusiasts of Smokey are also invited to help his campaign by becoming Junior Forest Rangers and to write to him at Smokey Bear Headquarters, Washington, D.C., 20252.

SOOTY
(Great Britain, b. 1948)
Sooty, the mischievous teddy bear glove puppet, is almost half a century old and has a place in *The Guinness Book of Records* as 'the most enduring puppet ever'. His TV show, *Sooty's Amazing Adventures*, is shown all around the world, and he has for generations been an accomplished stage performer. Bought in a gift shop at Blackpool in 1948 by amateur magician Harry Corbett while he was on holiday with his family, the bear was named 'Teddy' and was intended to be just a prop for use at children's parties. Instead, Harry started to use the puppet in his magic act, and when the pair appeared on a TV show, *Talent Night*, they proved the biggest hit of the evening. Thereafter followed regular spots on the children's show *Saturday Special*, before Harry decided to make 'Teddy' more distinctive for the small screen. He blackened the bear's nose and ears, renamed him Sooty, and the rest is history. For the next two decades the pair were rarely off the screen, in one series after another, and the Sooty models made by Chad Valley were best-sellers. Sadly, in 1975 Harry Corbett died following a heart attack, but the show went on with his son, Matthew, taking over. This duo continued until June 1996 when Matthew decided to sell Sooty, along with his inseparable companions Sweep and Soo, to the merchant bankers Guinness Mahon, for £1.4 million. Fans can be sure, however, that they will see a lot more of the little nylon orange bear in the future.

STUBBINS
(Great Britain, b. 1935)

Stubbins is a toy bear who lives with a group of other bear friends at Stubbington Manor, the country home of the rather pompous Lord Rushington. Almost koala-like in appearance, these bears, drawn by Dorothy Burroughes, feature in a series of books written by Lady Elizabeth Gorrell during the 1930s and '40s. Among the other characters in the group who tangled with all manner of humans, ranging from difficult shopkeepers to Americans billeted at Stubbington Manor during wartime, were Albert, Velvet Trousers, Sleepie, Golden Syrup, Orange Pekoe and the irrepressible little Bitty.

SUPER TED
(Great Britain, b. 1978)

Super Ted is another recent teddy bear success story: the little bear who combines the qualities of lovable ted and super-hero has seen his adventures translated into 15 languages and his TV show screened all over the world. He was created in Wales by Mike Young when he was trying to get his young son, Richard, off to sleep one night. 'The trouble was Richard was afraid of the dark,' recalls Mike, 'and I was forever trying to think up stories to take his mind off it. And then suddenly I got this bit of inspiration from the teddy bear that Richard was clutching. I had this idea of a teddy bear who was also afraid of the dark, but who could say magic words, peel off his fur, reveal a flying suit and cape, and go off on all sorts of adventures to help people and animals. Richard loved it and I had to keep making up stories about Super Ted, as I

named him.' Sensing that other children might share his son's love of the little bear, Mike and his wife, Liz, decided to set up their own business to publish stories about Super Ted and make models of the character for sale. Major success was achieved when *Super Ted* was turned into a hit TV series in 1982 and the Walt Disney organisation snapped up the rights for America. The R. Dakin company have since been licensed to make Super Ted in the United States; their version is unjointed but like the British bear has a Superman-style suit and an additional outer fur coat that can be unzipped and removed. The little bionic bear is also being merchandised on caps, bags, T-shirts, and, of course, pyjamas.

TEDDY EDWARD
(Great Britain, 1962)

Teddy Edward has been called 'the world's most travelled teddy' and was for years a star of the television programme 'Watch With Mother'. He is unique among teddies in having his adventures told in photographs taken by Patrick and Mollie Matthews. The original Teddy Edward, who made his debut in a book in 1962, actually belonged to the Matthews' daughter, Sarah, and it was her suggestion that her father, a photographer, should take pictures of the teddy and his friends and her mother should recount their adventures. So successful and highly praised were the subsequent books— Enid Blyton said of them, 'Teddy Edward seems to do all the things that every child would want their own teddy bears to

do'—that an industry grew up around the little bear and sent Patrick and Mollie on increasingly longer journeys to find locations for their stories. Among the places Teddy Edward visited were such exotic spots as Spain, Greece, India, Nepal, Bermuda and even the Sahara Desert. So demanding were these tours that a second bear had to be obtained to stand in for Teddy Edward, and in order to make the newcomer exactly like the original, he was required to undergo 'fur surgery' at the Hammersmith Dolls' Hospital. Later, the original 'retired' to a place of honour in Sarah's bedroom. The success of the TV series (begun in 1965), narrated by Richard Baker and seen in countries as far apart as Albania, Norway and New Zealand, resulted in still more spin-offs including postcards, cassettes and a picture strip in the weekly magazine *See-Saw*. In December 1996 Teddy Edward fetched £34,500 at a Christie's auction in London—seven times more than expected—when he was bought by toy company president Yoshiro Sekiguchi, to spend the rest of his days as the centre-piece of a museum in Japan.

TEDDY ROBINSON
(Great Britain, b. 1953)

Teddy Robinson started his life as just an ordinary teddy bear until his young owner, Deborah Robinson, took him to school and her teacher immediately gave him the name which is now familiar to his many admirers. It was Deborah's mother, Mrs Joan G. Robinson, who then decided to write some stories about the little bear and the adventures he shared with her daughter. Although nothing happens to Teddy until Deborah actually takes him somewhere, it is never very long before he is into some scrape or other, and apart from getting lost more than once he has also had a very dramatic encounter in a hospital! A lot of the Teddy Robinson stories are based on real incidents, and it seems almost a miracle that the original bear has survived to this day. He is now apparently much loved by Deborah's own family.

WINNIE-THE-POOH
(Great Britain, b. 1926)

Probably the most famous teddy bear in the world, Winnie-the-Pooh is known to children everywhere, his adventures by A. A. Milne having been translated into twenty-two languages (including Latin, Esperanto and the Initial Teaching Alphabet), and in the United States alone the book *Winnie-the-Pooh* has sold over fifteen million copies since it was first published. Almost a million copies have also been sold in Russia where he is known as 'Vinni-Pukh', and in the United Kingdom annual sales in paperback regularly exceed 100,000 copies. The honey-loving bear is based on a real teddy which was bought at Harrods in 1921 and was probably made by J. K. Farnell who had an exclusive contract with the London store. He was called 'Edward Bear' by Milne's son, Christopher, but renamed for the book 'Winnie', from an American black bear at London Zoo, and 'Pooh' after a favourite swan the Milne family knew at Angmering in Sussex. Numerous Pooh bears have been produced, based on the original book illustrations by Ernest Shepard (which, incidentally, he based on his own son's teddy, a Steiff bear named 'Growler'), including examples by The Teddy Bear Toy Company, Chad Valley, F. W. Woolnough, Sears, Roebuck & Company and Agnes Brush. For years there was a long-running BBC radio programme, *Children's Hour*, which regularly featured Winnie-the-Pooh, and since 1966 Walt Disney has made three cartoon films with a somewhat updated and plumper bear who wears a little red jacket. Amongst the host of items of merchandising can be found everything from pencil cases to (naturally) jars of honey. The original Winnie-the-Pooh now has a place of honour in the children's room of New York Public Library, where he is visited by millions of fans of all ages every year.

7

THE TRUTH ABOUT WINNIE-THE-POOH

In his autobiography, *It's Too Late Now*, published in 1939, A. A. Milne (1882–1956) says that there were two major influences on him in writing the stories about Winnie-the-Pooh— apart from the teddy bear bought at Harrods. The first was the book *Uncle Remus* which had been read to him as a child by his father: it was a story he never forgot. The second was the writer Rose Fyleman who first encouraged him to write for children and published some of the verses which later became *When We Were Very Young* (1924).

In his autobiography Milne tells an interesting story about this collection: 'One day when Daphne went up to the nursery, Pooh was missing from the dinner table which he always graced. She asked where he was. "Behind the ottoman" replied his owner coldly. "Face downwards. He said he didn't like *When We Were Very Young*." Pooh's jealousy was natural. He could never quite catch up with the verses.'

Whether Miss Fyleman played any part in the actual creation of *Winnie-the-Pooh* it is impossible to say, but prior to the appearance of Milne's famous work in 1926, she had herself written a short story about a teddy bear which was published in the London evening newspaper, *The Star*. It is interesting to speculate whether Milne had read 'The Vain Teddy' which is reprinted here for the first time. The story is followed by an article, published in the *Sunday Express* on 26 June, 1966, by Robert Pitman, the paper's literary editor, which attempts to throw further light on this intriguing mystery.

*   *   *

A.A. Milne with his son, Christopher Robin, and the teddy bear bought at Harrods which started the Winnie-the-Pooh cult.

THE VAIN TEDDY

There was once a toy Teddy-bear who belonged to a little girl called Peggy. He was very big, almost as big as Peggy herself, and I am sorry to say that he was very vain.

You see, people always said, when they saw him, 'What a beautiful Teddy-bear!'

Peggy thought there was no one like him in the world. He always wore a blue bow, and she even made a blue silk cap for him, which he wore on the top of his head. It really made him look rather ridiculous, but it had a feather in it, and the vain Teddy thought it suited him beautifully, though he would have preferred pink.

'Pink is really my colour', he said to himself. 'I wish Peggy would realise how well I should look in pink.'

He grew more and more conceited every day. The other toys didn't like him at all. He used to sit in the corner and never join in their talk. If anyone spoke to him, he just said 'Yes' or 'No', in a proud voice, and stared at the ceiling.

But he was punished in the end.

One day Peggy's mother bought a packet of pink dye for Peggy's Sunday frock (which had faded very badly in the sun), mixed it in a great big pot, and left it standing on the kitchen table.

The Teddy-bear was sitting on the window-sill just over the table.

'How pretty that dye is!' he thought. 'What a lovely colour! If only my cap were that colour, how handsome I should look!'

Then he had an idea. 'If I lean over', he thought, 'my cap will drop in, and then it will get dyed.'

He leaned over.

'Mind! Mind!' sang the canary.

But he took no notice. He leaned over farther and farther. Suddenly—splash! splash! He had fallen right into the pot of dye!

You never saw such a comical sight as he was when they got him out. Pink all over! Peggy still loved him as much as ever, but his appearance was utterly spoiled.

'What a funny Teddy!' people said now. In time he got used to it, but he never really got over it. He was never known to squeak again.

THE IMMORTAL POOH

One day forty-five years ago a pretty young woman went to Harrods and bought a teddy bear for her son's first birthday. The bear had an astonishing future in front of it.

At a big luncheon last week held in the bear's honour at the Dorchester, a cheque was presented to the *millionth* child for whom a copy of last October's paperback book about the bear was bought in just the few months since then. A little mental arithmetic will give you some idea of the steady annual value of the bear. The bear has become an industry.

As for the original animal itself, patched and resewn, it lies in a showcase in New York, as revered and honoured as a bust of Henry Ford in Detroit. It is, of course, Winnie-the-Pooh, the central figure of the stories which the late A. A. Milne wrote about his son, Christopher Robin.

We all know about Christopher Robin and Pooh. Or do we? During the past few weeks I have been investigating the facts about Pooh. It seems to me that, despite all the admiration and publicity, the full story has never been told. It is, I think you may agree, both sad and mystifying.

First, let us look at the accepted accounts of what happened to the toy bear when it was brought home from Harrods. At the time A. A. Milne was 38, and his wife Daphne was some ten years younger. He was a successful playwright, but he

was no John Osborne. He was modest, gentle, ever bubbling with a quiet stream of bizarre humour. This humour, we are told, soon began to flow around the fat, furry shape of the teddy bear from Harrods.

One day young Christopher Robin came down from the nursery when the actor Nigel Playfair was visiting. In a gruff voice the boy said, 'What a funny man. What a funny red face.' But he denied saying the words himself. He said it was his toy bear, whom he called Pooh, speaking.

Thus Pooh came to life—along with the boy's other toys, a piglet (bought by friends), a stuffed donkey, a tiger. Adult visitors, when invited, would ask, 'I suppose Pooh is going to be there?'

Milne began writing about Pooh. His wife has recalled: 'We were all acting little incidents with Pooh and the nursery animals the whole time . . . we were all quite idiotic about it. The animals had become very important to us.'

Mrs Milne has described how Christopher Robin would tell his father: 'Come and see me in my bath. And then you can read the latest story to Pooh.' In her words, 'Even when we were working we had fun in a world of special intimacy and utter silliness, laughing at ridiculous jokes and talking in our

(Above and opposite page) E. H. Shepard did not base his illustrations of Winnie-the-Pooh on Christopher Robin Milne's teddy, but on his own son Graham's bear, Growler. The sale of this piece of artwork for £1,200 (estimate £800) at Sotheby's on 5 February, 1968, inspired the *Punch* pastiche reprinted here.

own special language. Looking back to those days I always see Pooh and the small boy with whom we shared them . . . with his large brown eyes and beautiful corn-coloured hair cut square.'

Yet is this the whole story? In 1952 when A. A. Milne was lying ill with only four more years to live, a curious thing occurred. His son, Christopher Robin Milne, then 32, wrote in an article entitled 'Father':

'Strangely enough, although my father wrote so much about me, he did not like children . . . in fact, he had as little to do with children as possible. I was his only child and I lived upstairs in the nursery with my nanny. I saw very little of him. It was my mother who used to come and play in the nursery with me and tell him about the things I thought and did. It was she who provided most of the material for my father's books . . .'

About the Pooh stories, C. R. Milne declared: 'As far as I can remember I knew nothing of the stories until they were published. Then my nanny used to read them to me . . .'

Was the son being fair to his father? We know that as he grew older the boy hated the idea of being the Christopher Robin of the stories and being teased at school with, 'Where's your Teddy Bear?'

But, though unfortunately timed, his article made clear that, in his view, his father was a kind and delightful man. A typical moment: Once, wrote C. R. Milne, 'he found me sitting at the lunch table holding a fork upright . . . Instead of saying, "That isn't the correct way to hold a fork," he merely remarked, "I shouldn't do it that way if I were you. If someone fell through the ceiling, they'd fall on to the prongs and that would hurt them!"'

But what *is* the truth about the writing of the immortal Pooh stories? C. R. Milne now runs a small bookshop in the

West Country. Having written his article, he has said little about his father or himself and now politely refuses to say anything at all. Instead I have just visited his mother, Daphne Milne, at her flat high above Green Park in Piccadilly.

She explained to me why she has moved from the Sussex home in Ashdown Forest where the Pooh stories are set. It was because she had lost the housekeeper who had been with the family since Pooh was bought. She told me how she first met her husband.

'It was at my coming-out dance when I was 17. My god-father, Owen Seaman, who was editor of *Punch*, asked me if he could bring along one of his writers, A. A. Milne. I had always read and admired A. A. Milne's articles, so I said, "Of course."

'Life was so elegant then. It's the absence of servants that's made all the difference don't you think? My husband took a toy mascot, a dog called Carmen, to look after him in the First World War. He was saved from the Somme by trench fever. He wrote to say that Carmen had found a French germ up the trench and blown it on to him. Four years after that Christopher Robin was born.

'My husband dictated the stories to me. I didn't type or anything, but he needed an audience to react. He would walk to and fro puffing at his pipe while I wrote and laughed.'

I mentioned Christopher Robin's claim that he never heard the stories until they were in book form. 'Really?' said his mother. 'Oh, no. They were part of our lives.'

Copies of the Pooh books in every language line the shelves in Mrs Milne's exquisite flat. But she is hardly an old lady living in the past. In her seventies she is still decidedly attractive, vivacious, chic, and an active theatregoer.

One thinks of the laughing amateur secretary taking down A. A. Milne's dictation, and one also remembers what he himself says about his writing—namely that it was never sentimental, that all the characters in Pooh are in fact selfish and as tough as nails, that even the little boy in 'Christopher

The very collectable volume of songs by A. A. Milne and H. Fraser-Simson was also illustrated by E. H. Shepard.

Robin is saying his Prayers' is actually as egocentric and unfettered by morals as any other young animal.

Were these stories written primarily for a child at all? Or were they, in effect, written for the delight of the child's mother? It is an ironic thought.

Perhaps there is a sadness in the Pooh stories, the sense of a dream existence poised uncertainly on the edge of the harsh real world, which has helped to make them immortal.

8

COMICAL TEDDY BEARS

In this chapter Denis Gifford, creator of the British television cartoon series 'Quick On The Draw', and President of the Association of Comics Enthusiasts, leafs through the world's largest comic collection to consider the history of teddy bears in the strips. This is what he has discovered:

Many a bowl of Honey Puffs must have curdled in their cream that wet Wednesday morning of November the fourteenth, 1979. The dread headline blazed across *The Sun*, a dark spot clouding the Tenth Happy Birthday Week celebrations of Britain's best-selling newspaper. John Hill, ace newshound, reporting: 'Sad news, chums. Biffo the Bear has fallen on grisly times. His bosses on the *Beano* comic decided he is no longer a star—and have suspended him for two months. The long-running adventures of Biffo, once Britain's best-loved cartoon character, have been pushed out (can you bear it?) by Christmas advertising.'

A 'Shock-Horror!' report indeed: but *The Sun* was late with the news. *The Guardian* had broken the story the previous day, but regular readers of *The Beano* had already been without their Biffo for three long weeks. His last dated appearance was on October 27th. Very different treatment from the fanfare that heralded his arrival on the full-colour front page of January 24th, 1948. 'Hip Hurray! Biffo the Bear is Here Today!'

The little black bear in the red button-down pants was the creation of the late Dudley D. Watkins, who has probably been revolving in his Dundee grave since the day they displaced Biffo with Dennis the Menace. It was on September 14th 1974 that this earth-shaking shift occurred, marking the moment in time when British comic heroes switched from our four-legged friends to our two-legged enemies. Funny animals had lost the day and Spotty 'Erberts taken over!

As President of the Association of Comics Enthusiasts, the only club for British comic collectors, I was invited to comment. *The Sun* gave a succinct précis of my peroration: Yesterday author and children's comics expert Denis Gifford stuck

Biffo the Bear, perhaps the most famous of all comic strip characters, has been enjoyed by generations of readers of the *Beano*.

up for Biffo and said: 'I think he is suffering because he is an animal. Publishers seem to have decided that readers want to identify with the hero. That means boys and girls reading about boys and girls. I think they are out of touch with their readers. The comics will get very boring.' In other words, as I pointed out in radio interviews, there just aren't enough bears reading comics these days.

The nationwide interest shown by modern media in the suspension of a strip cartoon character from a kid's comic will be dismissed by many as typically trivial. The rest of us know better: the life of a cartoon character is more than just ink on paper. Biffo the Bear and his chums became part of the million memories belonging to generations of children. Favourite funny-folk live within us long after we grow out of our comic weeklies, and become as precious to us as our cuddlier companions of the cot. Which brings us to the subject of teddy bears.

Biffo the Bear was (hark at me! I mean, *is —*) not a teddy in the true sense of the term. He bears not the tell-tale dots at the shoulders and hips that mark the *genus teddius bearus* of the comic strip kind. But after all, teddy-type bears began with real bears—and so, of course, did the strip kind. The first cartoon bears made their debut in an American newspaper, the *San Francisco Examiner*, on June 2nd, 1895. A panelful of black and white bear cubs bustled about their business, drawn by Jimmy Swinnerton, destined to become the daddy of the American Sunday Funnies. Jimmy's 'Little Bears' went into colour in 1897, then took the trip to New York with him when Swinnerton was hired by press magnate William Randolph Hearst.

The 'Little Bears' predate the birth of the teddy bears, of course, as does the first British bear in comics, Billy Bruin. Billy was one of the mixed menagerie who made up 'Mrs Hippo's Kindergarten', the first strip ever to be published in the *Daily Mirror*. Unfortunately for Billy, April 16th, 1904 is better remembered as the birthday of his cartoon classmate, the character who was to emerge from Julius Stafford Baker's crowded panels as the star of the strip—Tiger Tim! After their newspaper debut, Billy, Tim and the rest of the jungle gang moved from the *Mirror* to star in colour in *The Playbox*, the comic supplement to a monthly magazine called *The World and his Wife*. In 1914 they transferred to the front page of a new comic, christened *Rainbow* in honour of its bright colours, where much to their myriad admirers' amazement, Mrs Hippo was transmogrified into Mrs Bruin: a great day for bear lovers everywhere. With the assorted animals re-christened 'The Bruin Boys', Tiger Tim and Co took on a new lease of life, and function to this day within the weekly pages of a comic called *Jack and Jill*. As Tim and his pals often remark, 'Hurray for Mrs Bruin!'

The first true teddy bear strip appeared as a page in the American weekly magazine, *Judge*. The year was 1907 and the cartoonist John Randolph Bray. 'Little Johnny and the Teddy Bears' starred a small boy and his even smaller pets, six little teds who sported a variety of hats, bow-ties, and pullovers. Their popularity was such that the Thomas A. Edison Company was inspired to produce a trick film called *The Teddy Bears*, in which a number of toy teddies were put through their animated paces in a primitive stop-frame

The very first cartoon strip featuring teddy bears, 'Little Johnny and the Teddy Bears', drawn by John Randolph Bray for the American magazine *Judge* in 1907.

An early British teddy bear strip, 'Bobby and the Woolly Bears', which ran in *The Butterfly* from August 1908.

system. This film in turn inspired J. R. Bray to try animating his own cartoon characters, and that led to a completely new career as America's first successful animated cartoon producer.

Meanwhile, this side of the sea at 25 Bouverie Street, London, the editor of *The Butterfly* was equally inspired. This weekly comic on green paper was already running a strip called 'Little Willie Winks and his Toy City', by Joe Hardman. Little Willie had a collection of magical toys which got up to all manner of mischief. There was a golliwog, a soldier, a couple of wooden dolls—and two teddy bears, one black and one white. But such was the contemporary craze for these lovable toys that when he saw Bray's strip in *Judge*, our jovial editor promptly commissioned one of his cartoonists to crib it! Consequently, 'Bobby and the Woolly Bears' burst happily onto the centre spread of *Butterfly* on August 22nd, 1908, quite unconcerned about Willy Winks and his Bears on the opposite page, and definitely unconcerned about Little Johnny and his Teddies in *Judge*! To complete the British boom in bears,

TEDDY, "THE TERROR" OF JUNGLEVILLE SCHOOL.

'Teddy the Terror of Jungleville School', another early British series which appeared in the *Family Journal* in 1909.

'Teddy the Terror of Jungleville School' arrived in *The Family Journal* 'Playground' feature on May 8th, 1909. 'The naughtiest scholar in the school' promptly upset the teacher, Miss Giraffe, by upsetting the blackboard on her nose! 'Oh dear! Miss Giraffe was angry! "Teddy, you are expelled!" she cried; while Hippo, the head boy, showed Teddy the quickest way home. But he's sure to be here again next week, Chicks!'

And he was! Ten years later Teddy the Terror was still at it, but better drawn. Herbert Foxwell, who had taken over J. S. Baker's 'Bruin Boys', took over Teddy, too. This was 1919, the year peace came to the people and the comics bloomed again. 'The Teddies', drawn by the prominent children's artist

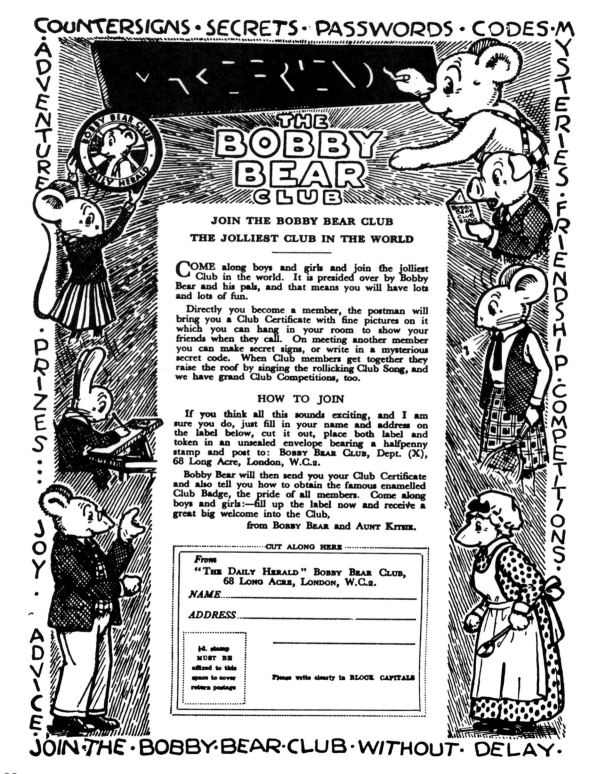

(Opposite) The *Daily Herald*
turned their comic strip hero,
Bobby Bear, into a children's
favourite in the Twenties and
later founded a club for readers.

Harry B. Neilson, brought much-needed fun to the pages of
the curiously titled comic, *The Sunday Fairy*. A title change to
The Children's Fairy failed to help, and that was the end of
Neilson's Teddies. Another new comic, and much more successful, was *Playtime*, with its assortment of nursery-style
characters including 'Bobby Bear'. But apparently the Editor
of the new left-wing newspaper *The Daily Herald* was not
numbered among the readers of *Playtime*. For in his own
Number One, published on March 31st 1919, just two days
after No. 1 of *Playtime*, under the title 'Picture Books for the
Bairns', who should appear in a cartoon but 'Bobby Bear'!

Here's a tale of Bobby Bear,
(See he's standing by the door);
As he meets his mother's stare,
Well he knows what is in store.
For breakfast time is sharp at eight,
And Bobby Bear is *always* late!

Aunt Kitsie (a Miss Bridges) added a P.S. to the first of her
'Little Talks' to young *Daily Herald* readers. 'I want all of you
Kiddies to write to me and tell me what you think of our
little Bear, and how you like painting the picture.' Well, all
the Kiddies liked him very much, and by the end of 1920 the
first collection of Bobby Bear cartoons was on sale for six-
pence. Two years later it became *The Bobby Bear Annual*, under
which title it came out every Christmas well into the 1950s,
long after the daily strip had ceased to be. Bobby Bear wrote
his own introduction to his first Annual: 'I must say it is a
very grate privilidge for me to have a rele book ritten about
miself, but I have alwaze been avery forchnit little bear, tho
I have my trubbles to, as you will see in this book. I hope all
who rede my advenchurs will injoy them as mutch as I did
miself.'

They certainly did, and when the inevitable happened and
a Bobby Bear Club was formed, by 1932 the membership
clocked a total of four hundred thousand children! Bobby
Bear rose to even greater heights of popularity when the
panel-and-caption format was changed to a proper daily strip,
first drawn by Wilfred Haughton (who also drew the *Mickey
Mouse Annuals)*, and later by the more stylish Rick Elmes.
Somewhat eclipsed today by the continuing success of the
Daily Express bear 'Rupert' (see elsewhere in this book), Bobby
deserves a place in history as the first bear in British
newspapers.

But for my own money, or honey, the favourite of all the
newspaper bears has to be 'Happy', the cute little cub who
so stole the scene in a strip called 'The Adventures of the

(Opposite) The enduring favourite, Rupert, who has been a feature in the *Daily Express* since 1920.

Noah Family' in *The Daily News* that cartoonist J. F. Horrabin just had to change the title to 'Japhet and Happy'. Boy and bear co-starred cosily from 1924 all the way to the Fifties. Before we leave the newspaper world altogether, a quick flip to 1935 and a swift glance at the short-lived 'Timothy Tar of *The Star*', who appeared in that paper's 'Peter Pan's Corner'. A serial strip by an artist called Breary, Timothy was reborn in the Fifties as 'Teddy Tar', star of several pocket-priced booklets put out by comic publisher L. Miller.

The teddy known as 'Timothy Tar', complete with shoulder and thigh studs, was a popular character in the *Star* in the mid-Thirties. Later, in the Fifties, he was renamed 'Teddy Tar'.

Meanwhile, back in the comics, teddies toddled amiably along. Arthur White, veteran from the Nineties who would still be at it in the Fifties, drew 'Teddy Tales' in *Chicks' Own* in 1920. Perhaps it would be more correct to say he drew 'Ted-dy Tales', for *Chicks' Own* was that educational oddity, a hyphenated comic. Walter Bell, on his way to becoming a veteran (still at it in the Seventies), began 'Bobbie and his Teddy Bears' for *The Sunbeam* in 1928. And Herbert Foxwell, not content with his previously mentioned entries, added 'Goldylocks and the Three Bears' to his output in 1920; they appeared in *Tiger Tim's Weekly*. Foxwell was the artist who linked comics and newspaper, when he created the weekly 'Teddy Tail' comic supplement for *The Daily Mail*. As there was no bear in the Mrs Whisker mouse household, Foxwell promptly produced 'Cubby and Lulu', a comical couple of cubs, for the 'Jolly Jack' companion comic given free with *The Sunday Dispatch*. As if to even things up, Harry Folkard, son of the originator of 'Teddy Tail', drew a bear strip called 'Paddy Polar' in the *Teddy Tail* comic, and the *Daily Express* promptly put a 'Rupert Bear' strip in their own comic supplement. All this in 1933.

The Thirties was the Golden Age for British comics; indeed, all forms of juvenile publishing flourished. One of the nicest, and today rarest, was a pocket-sized publication put out by John Leng of Dundee. This was *Fairyland Tales*, a weekly mixture of strips and stories aimed at the 'read-to-me-mummy' group. Among the regular favourites was 'Popinjay', a toy teddy who lived in Anthony and Rosemary's nursery along with his chum Wogga the Golly, Jiminy the Spaniel, and an occasional teddy-friend called Pongo. Popinjay had but to hear the call of his friend Adolphus, the teddy bear from down the road, and he was down the drain-pipe in a trice and off on more merry adventures. The illustrator of these anonymous tales was Sam Fair, who turned strip cartoonist in 1938 for Thomson's new comic, *The Dandy*. His character? 'Teddy Bear—The Grizzly Growler on the Prowl!' Popinjay attained some kind of collector's immortality in 1936 when he starred in *Popinjay's Jig-Puz Book*, a unique volume of five full-colour jig-saw puzzles, all for half-a-crown! The Thirties wound up in fine style with 'Sonny Bear and Mickey' arriving on the front page of *The Playbox*, delightfully drawn by Freddie Crompton; 'Bruno, Lionel and Percy Piggins' drawn by Fred Robinson for *The Golden*; and 'The Three Bears' in *Chicks' Own*, cartooned by Julius Stafford Baker's son, also named Julius.

The Forties were the Dark Ages for comics, with wartime paper shortages limiting size and circulation. Among the odder editions of the time there was *Cubby and the Christmas Star*, a 'Comic and Tracing Book' drawn by now famous comedian Bob Monkhouse, and a one-shot with the unlikely title of *Dizzling Comic*, which reprinted a Dutch strip called 'Terry and Berry the Bears' with a curious and pointless exhortation to 'cut them out, pin them to the wall, and have fun with them!' The decade ended brightly for bears, however, with the brilliant debut of good old Biffo in *The Beano*.

The Fifties saw a small boom in bears. *The Dandy*, not to be outdone by its comical companion, introduced 'Barney's Bear' in 1950. *The Beano* bounced back with 'Little Plum—

(*Opposite*) A. A. Milne's Winnie-the-Pooh first became a cartoon character in 1955, but his image was made radically different when Walt Disney secured the animation rights in 1979.

Your Redskin Chum', a strip by the very individual cartoonist Leo Baxendale. Plum's battles with some hungry bears became a recurring plot which so delighted both editor and readers that by the end of the decade they had spun off into their own strip, 'The Three Bears'. Hugh McNeill, best remembered for his 'Our Ernie' and 'Harold Hare', contributed to the canon by creating 'Teddy and Cuddly' for *Jack and Jill* in 1954.

The Fifties were also the first boom years for Children's Television, and the comics naturally began to reflect that boom. 'Andy Pandy' went onto the front page of the new comic *Robin* (1953), an attempt at producing a nursery school *Eagle*. Naturally the strip featured Andy's partner-in-prankishness, Teddy Bear. 'Sooty', the still-popular hand-puppet manipulated by performer Harry Corbett, made his first strip appearance in *TV Comic* (1954). The artist was Tony Hart, later a tele-personality in his own right, in his own series. When Sooty moved across to *Pippin* in 1967, the art chores were taken on by Fred Robinson, who continued to handle the strip beautifully in the combination comic *Pippin in Playland*. The year 1955 brought the first strip cartoon adaptation of A. A. Milne's 'Winnie the Pooh'. This was in the Ernest Shepard image, not Walt Disney's, and was delightfully drawn for *Playhour* by Peter Woolcock, the artist who had taken over 'The Bruin Boys'.

Television continued to dominate the Sixties, and Hanna-Barbera's 'Yogi Bear' opened the decade with a weekly appearance in *TV Land*. The artist, Chick Henderson, was English. This telly-cartoon character proved so popular that he won his own comic, *Yogi Bear's Own Weekly* (1962), which removed him from another paper he was appearing in at the time, *TV Express*. Yogi's comic was no wild success, and was merged into *Huckleberry Hound Weekly* in 1965. Yogi Bear pressed hungrily on, however, and turned up in 1972 in a high-priced paper called *Yogi and His Toy*. The price was high to cover the cost of a Grand Free Gift—every single week! Also from television came 'Tingha and Tucker', a couple of Koalas, who turned up in a comic called *Candy* in 1969. More teddified was 'Bearsworld', a strip in the same comic drawn by John Donnelly. Rolf Harris was another TV star to get himself involved with bears, and in 1966 both Rolf and 'Coojiebear' appeared in *TV Toyland*. That real life favourite from the Zoo, 'Pipaluk' the baby polar, popped into *Playland* in 1968. But there was a bit more punch in a character who turned up in 1965's *Storytime* . . . Superbear!

But undoubtedly the historic highspot of the Sixties, or indeed of the whole happy history of comics, as far as teddy bear fans are concerned, occurred on September 21st, 1963.

The first English comic entirely devoted to teddy bears was launched in 1963. *Teddy Bear* ran for ten years and special issues continued thereafter for almost a decade.

For on this day was published Number One of a comic wholly devoted to the doings of teddy bears and called, with utter appropriateness, *Teddy Bear*! Teddy himself edited the colourful comic from Bear Green, Farringdon Street, London, a site unbelievers may claim as the address of Fleetway House. Grand Free Gifts came with the first three issues, including 'My Magic Drawing Book', and as well as appearing on the cover of his comic, Teddy Bear starred in a two-page picture strip with the entire Bear family: Daddy Bear, Mummy Bear, Grandma Bear, Grizzly Bear, Snowy Bear, Bookworm Bear, Fred Bear (a tramp: get it?), Hill Billy Bear, Ivan Bear, and the baby of the family . . . Bare Bear! Among the fun, Teddy found time to deliver such honeyed homilies as 'Never interrupt Mummy when she is talking!' *Teddy Bear* ran for ten years, and still turns up annually in Summer Specials. Even this long life was beaten by 'The Teddy Bears', a strip which began in D. C. Thomson's *Bimbo* in 1961, transferred to *Little Star* in 1972, and bumbles merrily on.

The Seventies saw a decline in comic circulation as the television audience grew, but once again bears bridged the gap. 'Barnaby', created in foreign parts by one Olga Pouchine, was sufficient a hit on British TV to find a place as a strip in *Pippin*, where he was drawn by Jenny Reyn. 'Rupert', transferring to TV from the printed newspaper page, came into comics proper for the first time when *Pippin* started a run of reprints of the Alfred Bestall period, with the added plus of full colour.

'The Three Bears', created by D. C. Thomson, have appeared in both comics and paperbacks since the Seventies.

And 'Teddy Edward', another telly-puppet, turned up in the magazine *See-Saw* in the form of a photo-strip fumetti. Comics began to close almost as soon as they were launched, taking their teddies with them. New English Library brought out *Dusty Bear Monthly* in 1975, but even a Grand Free Dusty Bear Spaceman Badge failed to get it off the ground. *Toby*, dedicated to a dog but featuring 'Teddy in Toyland', was the first flop of 1976, closely followed by *Magic*. This should have succeeded superbly: well drawn, well coloured, it carried the adventures of 'Cuddly and Dudley', who were the naughty nephews, no less, of Biffo the Bear! But *Magic* folded, and the nephews disappeared, perhaps to make a place for their Uncle in the Great Comic in the Sky!

9

THE TEDDY BEAR CLUB

Teddy bear lovers and collectors have their own international organisation called Good Bears of the World which links arctophiles of every country in a giant 'hug' of friendship and dedication. The movement even has a special day each year, 27 October, the anniversary of President Roosevelt's birthday, which is known as 'Good Bear Day'. Celebrations, in particular Teddy Bears' Picnics, mark this occasion, and funds are also raised to enable GBW to continue its work of donating teddy bears to hospitals for young patients, to the elderly, and to all those who are felt to be in need of them. How this network of arctophilists has grown up makes an interesting story.

The tale goes back to the year 1951 when an American charity worker, Russell A. McLean, began to present teddy bears to his local hospital in Lima, Ohio. He was convinced of the toy's ability to cheer up and comfort sick children and infants, and hoped that in giving the bears he was providing—as he put it—'a little bit of Christmas spirit for youngsters every day of the year'. Such, indeed, was the success of his idea that it was soon spreading beyond the confines of Ohio, and McLean himself became affectionately known across America as 'The Teddy Bear Man'.

At the same time, a mounting interest in teddy bears was also being manifested across the Atlantic in Britain. In 1962 Colonel Bob Henderson, a long time devotee and student of the teddy bear, was nominated 'President of the Teddy Bear Club' for his work in emphasising the role of the teddy bear in western society.

The honour was a fitting one for a man who, as I know from my meetings with him, was an unlikely figure to have championed the cause of teddy bears. A tall, moustachioed career soldier who had been a regular army officer with the Royal Scots until his retirement in 1955, Colonel Henderson had first come into contact with teddy bears as a child when he was given a 1904 Steiff teddy. It was to prove the first in

a collection that would ultimately grow to over 600 and fill several rooms of his Edinburgh home. The Steiff, which was originally considered to be male, got the name by which 'she' is remembered, 'Teddy Girl', when Colonel Bob's young daughter, Cynthia, put her in a dress many years ago.

Colonel Henderson had a distinguished army career, serving on General Montgomery's staff during the Second World War, and keeping always at his side one special little bear who went with him right through the fighting.

'He was a miniature bear,' he told me, with a fond smile of remembrance. 'I kept him in my rucksack and he went absolutely everywhere with me. He was my link with home and happiness. I got a great deal of comfort from him and he helped me get through. Unfortunately, he didn't survive the war—he got so dusty he literally fell to pieces.'

Russell A. McLean, 'The Teddy Bear Man' who began the scheme for giving teddy bears to sick children in hospital.

(Opposite) Colonel Bob Henderson whose interest in teddy bears caused him to be nominated 'President of the Teddy Bear Club' in 1962. He is pictured holding Teddy Girl.

90

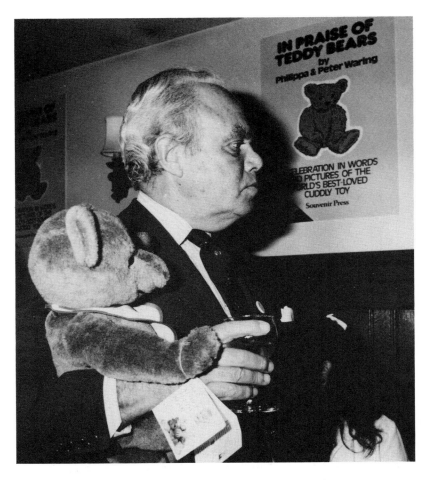

The actor Peter Bull, another influential figure in the growth of teddy bear awareness, pictured with Bully Bear.

At much the same time two authors were also gathering material for books: Margaret Hutchings, writer and toy maker, and Peter Bull, actor, traveller and author.

Margaret Hutching's *The Book of the Teddy Bear* appeared in 1964 and, apart from briefly recording the early history of the teddy bear, gave detailed instructions on how to make a whole variety of different and attractive teddy bears.

Peter Bull's book, however, was of a much more personal nature, and as his work in films and on the stage took him backwards and forwards across the Atlantic (he had important roles in *Dr Strangelove*, *Tom Jones* and the delightful *Dr Doolittle* as well as in notable plays like *Waiting for Godot* and *Luther*) he gathered together a wealth of stories about teddy bears. Following one appearance on the American TV show 'Today', he received over 2,000 letters from teddy bear owners. When his book *Bear With Me* appeared in 1969, he used it to explain the role of the teddy bear and went to

Peter Bull's famous miniature bear, Theodore.

considerable lengths to show that no one should be shy of confessing to owning one or loving one. Arctophiles, he said, were far more numerous than was supposed, and came from all walks of life, famous as well as ordinary folk.

'There's nothing childish about teddy bears!' I remember Peter Bull saying during one of our meetings at his comfortable King's Road flat in Chelsea, with his tiny friend 'Theodore' on one side of him and 'Delicatessen', later to become famous as 'Aloysius' in the TV production of *Brideshead Revisited*, on the other, as he used what I learned later was just one among many well-rehearsed, pungent yet affectionate comments on the subject: 'They are no more childish than collecting wives, cars or yachts.'

He made no secret of his obsession with teddy bears, which dated from his childhood and in particular from a dreadful incident when he returned home from school to find that his mother had given away his beloved teddy to a jumble sale. It was a story that he did not like repeating because of the painful memory.

'A lot of people have written to me over the years about their traumatic experiences when their teddy bears were taken from them as children—you must never do that,' he said. Despite his unhappiness, Peter Bull ultimately amassed more than 250 bears in his collection, and rather enjoyed the description of himself as 'looking something like a large, amiable bear'.

'Adults have a definite and equal need for teddy bears,' he told me. 'And think what they can do for you! The average bear doesn't mind being taken for a walk, dressed in ridiculous hats or even being read to. You can also blame him for anything and he won't deny it. I have always thought that a teddy is much cheaper than a psychiatrist, and not nearly as supercilious!'

Peter Bull was never in any doubt that there was a 'vast underground teddy bear movement' which would one day become very evident.

'But we arctophiles are a touchy lot,' he warned, 'and insults or ridicule by ignorant persons put our hackles up. One is teddy bear conscious in the same way other people are car, garden, clothes, food or cat conscious.'

Prompted by the work of these people on both sides of the Atlantic, teddy bears suddenly began to be featured in a whole variety of functions—at dances and on quiz programmes, at fairs and charity fêtes, and even as mascots at sports meetings and football matches. They also began to appear increasingly in newspapers, magazines and in advertisements.

Colonel Henderson, who had all the time been carefully

A sketch of some of Peter Bull's hug of bears.

studying this development of interest in the teddy bear, saw it as a phenomenon which he named 'Teddy Bear Consciousness'.

'It is so deep-seated in the unconscious depth of the mind that it is practically inherent in the human psyche,' he declared. 'It has given rise to the expression "The Teddy Bear Club" which thus exists in the subconscious mind and is something much more subtle than a cult. As has been seen it does from time to time come into conscious existence and practical activity at various places all over the world. All those who have an affection for teddy bears and those who love them, who appreciate the value of the teddy as an instrument in psychotherapy, and in this way are teddy bear conscious, are automatically members, though at first they may not realise it.'

As a result, explained Colonel Henderson, 'The Teddy Bear Club' has no subscription, no committee, no meeting place and no funds. It exists only universally in the subconscious mind, but an appreciation of the fact can be the first step towards bringing together those of a like mind into actual gatherings.

The year 1970 proved to be a most important one for the teddy bear, for it was then that what had hitherto been informal became formal with the founding of the Good Bears of the World in the United States.

The driving force behind this new movement was an American broadcaster and journalist, James T. Ownby, from

The symbol of Good Bears of the World.

James T. Ownby, the Founder and Chairman of Good Bears of the World.

Honolulu, who had been prompted to his action by Peter Bull's book *Bear With Me*, published that year in America under the title *The Teddy Bear Book*.

Like Peter Bull a big, amiable, rather bearlike man, he had fond memories of his own childhood teddy and, with a middle name of Theodore and a family story that the Ownbys were distantly related to President 'Teddy' Roosevelt, it seemed fated that he would become involved with the teddy movement.

'It was while I was reading Peter's book about teddy bears

96

and the warmth they can provide for the young and old that I had this inspiration,' he told me. 'That's what started me on the idea of people around the world expressing love and caring by making gifts of teddy bears. There is something endlessly appealing about the soft, cuddly little figure. So I decided to set up Good Bears of the World, a non-profit-making voluntary association dedicated to bringing together teddy bear lovers in America and the rest of the world to raise money to give this lovable toy to children in hospital. For if you're sick and lonely in a strange hospital bed, love *is* a teddy bear.

'It seemed to me that any group in any community anywhere in the world could set up their own "den", raise funds to buy bears or even make their own. Then have the pleasure of delivering them to folk in hospital and seeing the joy they bring. Teddy bear power is not only love for children and seniors, but for anyone who can appreciate the ideals we have for Good Bears of the World.'

Selecting the anniversary of President Roosevelt's birthday, 27 October, as a most appropriate day, and aided by Colonel Henderson, Jim Ownby founded GBW (as it subsequently became known), at a particularly suitable locality, Berne in Switzerland, 'Bear Town'. This was to be the headquarters of what he saw as an international humanitarian association pledged to form local groups (called dens) and raise money to buy teddy bears for sick children and those of any age in need of them. Each 27 October thereafter was to be marked as 'Good Bear Day'.

Such was the response to the new organisation that on 'Good Bear Day' 1973, it was officially inaugurated by a special gathering at the Bellevue Palace Hotel in Berne, after which the founders made a visit to the famous local *Bärengraben* (Bear Pits). In the subsequent newspaper reports of this event, one journalist wrote, 'The appeal of the teddy bear is universal. It is an international symbol of friendship and goodwill, and a bringer of comfort and affection in times of stress. Doctors say that Teddies do have considerable therapeutic value not only for children, but also for sick, lonely and elderly adults as well.' (As a matter of record, although Berne did continue as headquarters of GBW for some years thereafter, the centre was subsequently switched to Mr Ownby's home town of Honolulu in Hawaii. Following his death in 1986 it has been based in Ohio.)

Since 1973 GBW has grown on both sides of the Atlantic, recruiting new members all the time. Male members of the movement are known as 'Bearos', women as 'Bearines' and children as 'Cubs'. Today America has over 13,000 members, the United Kingdom over 1,000, and there are also members in

(Overleaf) The special Fall 1979 issue of the GBW magazine *Bear Tracks* was devoted to acknowledging the debt all teddy bear lovers owed to President Roosevelt.

4,000 Circulation This Issue

BEAR TRACKS

**OFFICIAL NEWSLETTER OF
THE GOOD BEARS OF THE WORLD**

Photo courtesy of the T.R. Association

THANK YOU TR!

**FALL
1979**

Canada, Australia, New Zealand, Germany, Austria, Norway, France, Switzerland, and numerous other places such as Hong Kong and Korea.

To the members of GBW who worked to establish the movement in the early days, their greatest triumph was undoubtedly 'The Great Teddy Bear Rally' held on 27 May, 1979, at Longleat in England, which was reported in the press throughout the world. Over 15,000 people turned up, accompanied by more than 2,000 teddy bears—many from abroad and places as far away as America, Europe, Australia and New Zealand—and during the day over 500 bears were donated to Dr Barnardo's Homes. Hard on the heels of this event, 'The First Teddy Bear Convention' was held in Auckland, New Zealand, on 23 August, and from 27 August to 9 September a group of Australians ran a similar rally in Bankstown Square, Sydney, which attracted huge crowds. Also in Australia, at Toowoomba, Queensland, a Teddy Bear Museum was opened. It now houses over 400 bears ranging in size from a few centimetres to three metres. Pride of the collection is a 73-year-old teddy made in London in 1906,

(Below and overleaf) Teddy Bear lover the Sixth Marquess of Bath, and the Marchioness, hosted 'The Great Teddy Bear Rally' at their home, Longleat, in May 1979.

BRING YOUR BEAR!

LONGLEAT
SUNDAY MAY 27th
THE GREAT TEDDY BEAR RALLY
and HONEY FAIR

LONGLEAT HONEY FAIR

TO THE GREAT LONGLEAT TEDDY BEAR RALLY

LONGLEAT — WARMINSTER — WILTSHIRE (between Bath & Salisbury on the A362) Telephone: Maiden Bradley 551

which is now regarded as 'The Oldest Teddy Bear in Australia'.

June 4, 1982 saw the first major American teddy bear rally at Philadelphia Zoo in Pennsylvania, which attracted 25,000 people and almost twice that many bears. It proved to be the start of a new teddy craze in the United States as further rallies were held across the country, attracting newspaper and magazine attention. In July of that year, the *New York Times* reported that 'teddy bears are everywhere and carrying one is, apparently, an invitation for a cuddle . . . the underworld of teddy bear lovers is surely out of the closet!'

In December 1984 *Newsweek* devoted four pages to what it described as the teddy bear phenomenon. 'It may be the era of electronic whizbangs,' said the magazine, 'but some of the best-selling software these days is teddy bears. US sales, about

(Opposite) Just a few of the 15,000 people – plus teddy bears – who attended The Great Teddy Bear Rally at Longleat.

100

Big Ted, believed to be the largest teddy bear in existence,
who has attended numerous rallies in recent years.

$40 million a year in the 1970s, swelled to $125 million last year, and retailers think the bear market will get even bigger in the future. More than 40 per cent of sales are *to* adults and *for* adults.'

A further acknowledgement of the affection in which the teddy bear is held came in 1985 in UNICEF's 'Year of Youth'. The international organisation reported that little Ted, who for years had been regarded as just a plaything, was now seen to epitomise carefree childhood. He was a perfect symbol for what became known as 'The Year of the Teddy Bear'— and confirmation, if any was still needed, of the important role of teddies in the contemporary world.

Ten years later, in 1995, the American Good Bears of the World celebrated their 25th anniversary with rallies and special appeals which enabled them to present a record number of bears to sick children and adults. In 1998, the British branch will mark its quarter-century from the gathering in Berne in October 1973 with similar special events on this side of the Atlantic.

10

THE FANTASTIC APPEAL OF THE TEDDY BEAR

Colonel Bob Henderson devoted his life to investigating the reasons *why* the teddy bear has come to have such a unique influence upon human emotions. This essay was written for the original edition of the book and is still regarded as one of the earliest and most authoritative statements on the subject.

In her book *A History of Toys*, Lady Antonia Fraser asks, 'What is it about the teddy bear which gives it this fantastic appeal? This is without doubt one of the most interesting psychological questions about the history of toys.' Also, in *The Book of the Teddy Bear*, Margaret Hutchings said, 'the almost unfathomable appeal of the teddy bear is universal and to all ages'. While Peter Bull, in his book *Bear With Me*, said, 'Teddy bears seem destined to survive everything and emerge as a triumphant symbol.'

Consequently, Mrs Eithne Kaiser, in her draft manuscript for a book on this subject, wrote

> This phenomenon is, in fact, so intense, so widespread, and so utterly taken for granted by adults, many of whom adhere to it themselves, that it demands some investigation both psychologically and mythologically for the bear, in the form of the teddy-bear has, oddly it seems, become our society's comforter. That almost all-pervading cuddly creature, which for many children is more important than any doll, and which remains with so many adults as something at once intrinsic and marginal to their most intimate life, acts *in loco parentis* as an archetypal mother/father understander-of-all, as indeed an original comforter, or Paraclete.

Funnily enough, a clue to the solution of this mystery was

Teddy Girl, Colonel Bob's life-long companion, was never far from his side.

quite lightheartedly though very rightly given by Peter Bull over the radio on 2 March, 1977, when he was having a talk with Pete Murray in the 'Open House' programme and got onto the subject of teddy bears. They both agreed that teddy bears talk to you. 'It is in the way they look at you' they said.

Now when you come to consider this, you realise that this experience is, in fact, a feeling within you that is aroused by your sight of the teddy bear, though it speaks to you only in the sense of the significance it has for you, and this is largely connected with its form, which is that of a bear cub, soft and cuddly, so it appeals to your hunting and maternal, or paternal, instincts.

The teddy does not, of course, actually speak to you. It only seems to do so, because in your mind you imagine it does. By means of its subtle appeal the teddy bear excites your imagination, so that its significance as a symbol is impressed

105

upon your inner consciousness. This region of your mind is where the archetypal Ideas in the realm of depth psychology assume symbolic form, which in our dreams often tend to take animal form, as they do in fairy tale and myth. Consequently, your vision of the teddy bear is linked in the depth of your mind almost automatically with the archetypal symbolic bear that has figured so largely in ancient mythology and is still active in this area of the mind. So you become inwardly involved in this psychological archetypal activity.

The influence of teddy bears can be beneficial to young and old, as this amusing cartoon by Larry Ross from a 1980 issue of *Time* magazine indicates.

As a symbol of love, affection and friendship the teddy bear appeals to the higher levels of your inner consciousness. This activates the better aspects of the universal archetypal symbolic bear (The Great Bear) and through this universal archetypal activity the teddy bear makes an appeal to the core of your inner being. This causes your inner voice to speak to your outer consciousness through the universal unconscious.

Consequently, when you are inwardly, or outwardly, talking to the teddy bear you are talking to your inner Self. The bear is merely the channel of this communication.

But, because your soul is linked with the Absolute, through this experience the 'personality' of the teddy bear can affect you in such a way that it puts you in touch with the Infinite. Indeed, one professional clinical psychologist, Floyd R. Clark, has maintained that in this way the gap between your conscious mind and the universal unconscious, or 'racial unconscious', is bridged, so that you are enabled spiritually to become aware of a universal unity in all things when you are properly attuned to it.

When this happens you are not worshipping the bear, but using it as a psychological instrument, or medium, that is capable of establishing such communication. In a sort of way it serves as a type of communion cup. One which will serve children well until they are old enough to partake in Christian Communion.

This is a perfectly natural thing to do, and is not in any way an abnormality. Those who consider arctophiles to be odd just do not realise this. The only peculiarity is the very personal reactions and associations in the experience, which are of course peculiar to each individual in the sense of belonging exclusively to them, not in the sense of being odd or strange.

So you see, the 'vast underground Teddy Bear movement' that Peter Bull says 'exists in the adult world' (see *Bear With Me*, page 88) is really a psychological movement in the mind rather than anything else. The factors underlying it lie far down in the realm of depth psychology; though largely concealed they are partly revealed in Jungian psychology.

I would explain it this way:

1 The subtle appeal of the teddy bear exercises your imagination, and this links your conscious mind, through the archetypal symbols in the collective unconscious, with the spiritual realm of divine Ideas.
2 The activity of these archetypal Ideas, that is the serialisation of creation, is inherent in all things, consequently images of them are engraved in the human soul, and reflected in the universal unconscious and express themselves through psychological archetypal activity.

(*Opposite*) The bionic Snoozy Bear, which can help soothe crying babies, was designed by Andrew Page in 1980.

3 The archetypal Idea of the bear, thus deepseated in the soul, is constantly represented by the archetypal symbolic bear in the collective unconscious.

4 As the teddy bear so well represents this archetypal symbolic bear, it is brought forward into the conscious mind, and so links the conscious mind with the divine archetypal Idea of the bear. The opening of this channel permits spiritual inspiration to flow through it.

5 The teddy bear is grasped in psychic compensation and clung to for security. In this way it provides satisfaction for a widespread psychological need. This takes it right out of the classification of a soft toy.

6 When the teddy bear is permitted to function in this way its significance can activate this psychological archetypal activity, and so have a powerful psychotherapeutic effect. This ultimately accounts for the fantastic appeal of the teddy bear, which derives from the absolute function of the archetypal bear, its function as a surrogate for the mother as comforter, and for the Holy Ghost as The Comforter. (This comes about through association with the Great Bear constellation—*Ursa Major*—which was believed to be a representation of the 'Great Mother'. In medieval Christian symbolism, for example, the archetypal symbolic bear was considered to be in close association with the Creator, and

Pudsey, the symbol of BBC TV's annual 'Children-in-Need' programme which raises millions of pounds for deserving causes. (Illustration by Brian Robson.)

to function as a symbol of both regeneration and resurrection.)

Thus, through its psychological links with both the instincts (hunting, maternal and paternal) and the inner knowledge of the soul (gnosis), and by means of the influential significance of the archetypal symbolic bear that it represents, the gift teddy bear can in many different ways serve as a powerful source of comfort, consolation and encouragement, and be highly effective as a gift of friendship, a token of love, a symbol of hidden strength, a transmitter of spiritual forces, as well as a pointer to unfolding perfection.

In so doing it can help to dispense 'a little bit of Christmas spirit' practically every day universally.

Finally, the important point to keep in mind is the fact that the teddy bear functions as a symbol. It is what it represents that counts. From the psychologist's point of view it is a representation of an 'archetypal' symbol in the form of a bear. From the mythologist's point of view it is a 'mythological' symbol in the form of an 'effect image' — that is, one which functions mystically.

C. G. Jung maintained that the imageries of mythology and religion serve positive life-furthering ends. They are energy releasing and directing signs, which inspire and move one in a particular way. That is why the gift teddy bear can function in many ways and bring to its owner feelings of security, contentment and happiness.

In this way teddy truly becomes a 'Good Bear of the World'.

11

A BEARISH MARKET

The worldwide growth of awareness about teddy bears during recent years—and especially in the years since this book first appeared—has made them very collectable and increasingly valuable. Where it was once unheard of for teddies to appear at auctions in the way that toys and dolls have done for many years, they have now become star attractions at these sales, frequently making newspaper headlines when rare examples are sold for record prices.

Of course, to many people the sentimental value of a bear cherished since childhood far outweighs what it might be worth to sell. But the fact remains that because the teddies which belonged to earlier generations of children—in particular the 'golden era' before the First World War and during the 1920s and '30s when so many exciting varieties were produced—have become far fewer in number, it is increasingly important to document the history of the manufacturers who produced them. Although most teddy bears were made in

Sale room
Teddy bear fetches top price

By Geraldine Norman
Sale

Sot
price
yeste
tedd
for
It h
sno
hu
dr
co
b
i

Sale room
Teddy bear prices give auctioneer a big surprise

an, Sale Room Correspondent

were also bought by Mr Wright and
and he paid £374 (estimate £60-
eiff, £100) for a similar straw-
with stuffed, plush teddy which
and Phillips had not attributed to a
ion named manufacturer.
ate The sale totalled £45,536
with nine per cent left unsold.
re The biggest moneyspinner at
o- Sotheby's was a Fabergé hard-
at stone figure of a carpenter
n testing the sharpness of his axe
e which sold for £82,500 (estimate £80,000-£100,000).
The curiosities of the Russian
sale lay in luxury
equipment sent

Sale room
Records fall on big day for early teddy bears

By Geraldine Norman, Sale Room Correspondent

Teddy bears had their big day at Sotheby's yesterday. An American private collector beat the previous auction record when he paid £2,310 for a Steiff beige plush bear dating from about 1910 and went on to beat his own record with a resounding £3,740 for another large Steiff silver plush bear of about 1905. The first had been estimated at £1,000 to £1,500 and the second at £800 to £1,200.

Teddies, which derive their name from President Teddy Roosevelt were first

dolls, a much longer-established collecting field. A charming "Uncle Tom" style Negro automaton doll, made by Gaston Vichy in France about 1880 sold for £9,680 (estimate £7,000 to £8,000) to a private collector. He is seated in a rocking chair wearing a straw hat and smoking a pipe. A Schmitt et Fils bisque doll of the same period went for £5,940 (estimate £4,000 to £6,000) to Mariko, a London dealer. Bonham's sale of Lalique

Teddy bears making news: *Times* newspaper reports (*previous page*), a photograph of some of the 75 bears auctioned at Christie's in February 1990, with the firm's expert, Philippa Spurrier (photo: Peter Trievnor/ Times Newspapers Ltd.); and *Daily Mail* cartoonist Mac's wry cartoon of 21 September, 1989.

'Oh, she's noticed, has she? Well, tell her daddy's taken them for nice walkies to Sotheby's.'

Bunny Campione, Doll and Teddy Bear Consultant, who organised the first teddy bear auction in 1982. She is holding a Steiff dual-plush bear, circa 1920, which sold for £55,000 in September 1989. Photo: Campione Fine Art.

quantity, enough have disappeared to give rarity value to the survivors. John Davies, in *The Times* in December 1990, pondered on where these bears might have gone: 'It has been suggested, quite seriously, that heavy casualties occurred during the Second World War. The two British obsessions of the time—constipation and germs—caused mothers to force-feed children with cod liver oil and kidnap teddy bears, which were then surreptitiously dumped as a health hazard ('Teddy's gone to fight that nasty Mr Hitler').

As a child who lost a much-loved 'Widdly Teddy' to such unscrupulous tactics, this is a view with which I have much sympathy, although there is no doubt that a great many more bears suffered from too much loving and a lot of other unfortunates were literally torn limb from paw by careless owners. Nowadays, it seems, an increasing number of adults who were parted from their childhood companions for one reason or another are among the throng collecting teddy bears with remarkable zeal.

One person who has been close to this phenomenon is Bunny Campione, teddy bear consultant, who organised the

113

An early Steiff bear, circa 1905, with a selection of the 'magic buttons' so important for authenticating the German firm's products.

first auction at Sotheby's in 1982 and has seen prices soar year after year ever since. She remembers that first sale very clearly.

'A client told me she had a collection of teddy bears she wished to sell and would I consider putting them up for auction? Let's see whether the market will take it, I thought. Approximately 25 teddy bears arrived at my office. Among them was a black bear with large ears and a rather pointed snout. His stuffing had shifted, causing his limbs and belly to flop around, giving him a forlorn look. Although I knew he was not by Steiff, the famous German maker, I suspected he might be a 1910 English bear, and he realised £460 which was the top price of the day. It was not until later that I discovered he was actually an American bear who had been made by the equally important Ideal Toy Company.'

Within a few years, the hundreds of pounds which those early bears fetched turned into thousands as age, maker and quality became more important to the larger and increasingly discerning market. Auctioneers and dealers also had to be on their guard against fake antique bears made by fixing the labels of leading manufacturers to unmarked examples. Because of this John Bly, another expert on toy collecting, says there are certain essential elements to look for when considering a bear as an investment. These are *age* and *make*, *colour* and *condition*, *shape* and *size*. He warns, though, against devoting too much energy to trying to find the rarest bears:

'Do not be obsessive looking for the magic button and lose sight of all the other lovely bears that can be bought for only a few pounds, for this is the best way to learn and form a collection. Talk to as many experts, both professional and amateur, as you can. Like all true enthusiasts, arctophiles love their chosen subject and are only too willing to impart their knowledge. Visit as many shops, auctions and fairs as you can. That there might just be an early retirement gift for you in your next local car-boot sale is something to bear in mind.'

Here, then, as an introduction, is some basic information on the major teddy bear manufacturers, their most successful products, and the best ways of identifying them. The prices which I have quoted are, of course, only estimates based on the figures reached at recent auctions and endorsed by the opinions of several dealers. Indeed, with the way that prices are rising at the moment, they may well already be under-estimates by the time this book is published!

At the time of writing, the world record price for a bear is £110,000 which was paid in 1996 by the Japanese collector, Yoshiro Sekiguchi, for the 1904 Steiff cinnamon-coloured bear

Christie's portrait of 'Teddy Girl' when she was sold for the world record figure of £110,000 in 1996. Now replicas of Colonel Bob Henderson's favourite bear are being marketed by her new Japanese owner.

'Teddy Girl' which had belonged to the late Colonel Bob Henderson. The news of the sale and the departure of 'Teddy Girl' to Japan was something of a sad moment for me because when I first started work on this book, back in 1979, I spent several happy days in her company and that of Colonel Bob at his home in Edinburgh. Indeed, I can still vividly remember the uncanny way her soft dark eyes seemed to follow me wherever I moved.

A year on, 'Teddy Girl's' new owner has produced a 2,000 limited edition replica for sale to collectors, with 150 being allocated to the United Kingdom via Teddy Bears of Witney. Costing £245 each, a total of only 500 examples have been exported from Japan. At the same time, Colonel Bob himself has also been honoured by Steiff with the launching of a curly, gold mohair bear named 'Henderson' and also sold by Teddy Bears of Witney in a limited edition of 2,000, with GBW receiving a donation from every sale. With typical Steiff long arms, big feet and a pronounced back hump, this very striking bear wears a distinctive Henderson tartan bow tie.

*   *   *

It would be wrong to think that children did not have model bears to play with before the birth of the teddy bear. In some parts of Europe, for generations, little replicas of the animal had been carved by woodsmen for their infants, and for just as long the bear may well have inspired needlewomen to create small replicas, although only a very few examples of either have survived in museums to the present day.

In the mid-nineteenth century, there is evidence that various kinds of *Bruin Bears* were being made of wood or of real fur stuffed with wood shavings. These rudimentary toys were intended to look just like bears in the wild and stood on all fours, had humped backs, a fierce expression and were either dark brown or black in colour. Most of these *Bruins* came from countries like France, Germany, Hungary and Russia, and were copies of the dancing bears which were dragged by their owners in chains and muzzles from town to town to entertain the local population. In the 1880s, some of the more ingenious toy manufacturers utilised clockwork mechanisms to make their model bears dance, raise a mug to their mouths, move about on wheels or even snap their jaws. It is hard to believe, however, that any little tots of the time would have particularly wanted to cuddle these bears!

Among the few companies known to have manufactured such bears were the French firm **Descampes** and **Gebrüder Sussenguth** of Coburg in Germany, who initially made dolls

Sketch of a mid nineteenth-century brown bear made in Germany.

and small toys. The Sussenguth models were known as *Peter Bears* and, although very rare nowadays, are remembered for their moving tongues, sharp, bared teeth and staring black glass eyes which rolled from side to side. They were evidently too ferocious-looking to be successful with children, and not many have survived. The last *Peter Bear* to be sold at auction in Germany was purchased by an American collector for the enviable figure of £8,000.

The first true teddy bears produced by Margarete Steiff and Morris Michtom in 1903 are, obviously, even more valuable, the Holy Grail of collectors. The early versions of both types are extremely rare, and those examples that do come onto the market tend to date from 1904 onwards, with the earliest in fine condition conservatively expected to fetch £20,000 at

(This page and overleaf) Two Steiff blond plush teddy bears, circa 1905, which were sold at Sotheby's in 1985 for record prices.

auction. The **Steiff** plush bears, with their long, curved limbs and spoon-shaped paws, are immediately identifiable by the firm's famous trademark. The earliest buttons from 1903–4 were embossed with an elephant; next followed a blank disc from 1904–5; and thereafter a stud stamped with the name Steiff with the tail of the last 'f' curling up under the word to end beneath the letter 'e'. By contrast, Morris Michtom's **Ideal Novelty and Toy Company** did not consider a label necessary for their jointed mohair plush bears with pointed snouts, and this has made authenticating some of their products difficult as well as providing an opportunity for the unscrupulous to create forgeries. The auction estimate for a typical Ideal teddy of around 1907 is at present £3,000.

Also highly sought-after are the novelty bears which Steiff produced from 1908 until the start of the First World War, among them the rare *Dancing Bear* (1908) which has a muzzle like the traditional bear, growls when its stomach is pushed, and in fine condition is valued at £10,000; the *Roly-Poly Bear* (1909) with a ball-shaped body that wobbles from side to side when touched and is now worth around £1,250; and the *Somersaulting Bear* (1912), driven by clockwork, which tumbles across the ground when its arms are twisted round to wind the motor. In good working condition, one of these bears may fetch around £2,000.

Among the first of the other German toy manufacturers to realise what a potential goldmine Steiff had discovered was **Gebrüder Bing** in Nuremberg. Founded by two brothers in 1865, the company had initially made tinplate products for the domestic market before adding a line of clockwork toys to their range at the turn of the century. Their first *Bing Bears* were small, mechanical animals that walked, somersaulted or played football. Well preserved examples are now valued at about £600. Around 1910 Bing began to produce more traditional mohair teddy bears with very rounded features and stumpy legs. Bing tried to copy Steiff by fixing a button trademark in the bears' ears, but their rivals promptly took legal action and they settled instead for an arrow tag. This, though, was not long in being replaced by a stud under the bear's arm, embossed with the letters 'GBN' (Gebrüder Bing, Nuremberg). A second revision to just 'BW' (Bing Werke) occurred in the early 1930s. Fine examples of pre-First World War *Bing Bears* can fetch over £800.

A second German manufacturer to start producing teddy bears was **Hermann**, founded at Sonneberg in 1907 by Johann Hermann. Already one of the world centres of toymaking, Sonneberg attracted buyers from all over the world, and Hermann sensed an opportunity to meet the growing demand for teddies—especially in America. The early Hermann bears

STEIFF PLUSH BEARS

To get a supply for Spring 1907, of this wonderful selling line, place orders now and insure delivery

An early American advertisement for Steiff plush bears from *Playthings* magazine, Autumn 1906.

were not unlike those of Steiff, although they had rounder heads and shorter muzzles that were often made from a different material from the rest of the toy's mohair plush. Hermann bears can be identified by a round metal tag displaying the letters 'BEHA' attached to the chest with a red cord. All this company's products are highly collectable and fetch in excess of £1,000.

The third major German company to emerge at this time was **Schuco**, the brainchild of youthful Heinrich Müller who went into partnership with an established toymaker, Albert

Schreyer, in 1912. The name Schuco was an abbreviation of Schreyer and Co and the firm started production with a line of mechanical bears and a series of little teddies just six centimetres (2½ inches) tall. These miniatures, known as *Mascot Bears*, consist of a tiny metal frame covered with short-pile mohair plush to which have been added felt paws and small, v-shaped feet. The company also introduced another very popular line, the honey-coloured mohair plush *Yes-No Bears*, each with a stumpy tail that functions as a lever to move the bear's head, signifying 'yes' or 'no'. These toys should carry a double-sided tag on their chests showing, on the reverse, a bear having its tail pulled, and on the front the words 'Schuco Patent Germany' with a rather curious-looking little boy clutching his legs! Today early Schuco miniatures can fetch up to £2,000 with the *Yes-No Bears* making about £500.

Not surprisingly, in America too there were several companies keen to cash in on the teddy bear craze. At the forefront was the colourfully named **Knickerbocker Toy Company** of New York which had been founded in the early 1900s. Their clipped mohair plush bears are notable for large, round heads, soft, cuddly limbs and almost flat, stubby features. They all carry a sewn-on label fitted into the bear's body seam, which shows the figure of a small child inside an inverted horseshoe and the words 'Animals of Distinction'. Fine examples of these bears have been valued at up to £1,000. During the 1920s Knickerbocker produced a black mohair bear with a triangular-shaped head and large, round ears, which can now realise up to £500 at auction, and they were also one of the firms licensed to produce the best-selling *Smokey Bear* toys.

What amounted to a cheeky bit of opportunism was perpetrated by the **Columbia Teddy Bears Company** when they introduced *Laughing Roosevelt* in 1908. Very similar in appearance to Morris Michtom's original 'Teddy's bear', this short, mohair plush bear with big paws and feet had in addition a mechanism hidden in its stomach which, when pressed, caused his mouth to open, exposing a complete set of shiny white glass teeth! Unfortunately, very few examples of *Roosevelt* have survived and good specimens are valued in excess of £3,000. Also much sought after are the teddies made by the exotically named **Fast Black Skirt Company**, which could growl, tumble and even play tunes. These bears can command upwards of £500, the most valuable being those that are provided with battery-operated eyes set in motion by pressing a button on the stomach.

English toy manufacturers were soon alert to the demand for teddy bears. Indeed, there is a claim that one of the best-known, **J. K. Farnell** of London, which had been making toys

121

Advertisement for the curiously named Fast Black Skirt Co. of New York whose teddy bears are now much sought after.

and dolls for years beforehand, actually 'invented' the teddy bear. The company, founded by Agnes Farnell in the mid-nineteenth century, since 1897 had been producing animal toys made from rabbit skins for sale on both sides of the Atlantic, and bears were certainly an item in their range. The curly mohair plush teddies which they made from the mid–1900s have long limbs, humped backs, sharply protruding muzzles and claws stitched onto their paws. Because they carried no trademark, early Farnell bears can be difficult to identify, but two examples which have been auctioned in recent years fetched £1,250 apiece. In 1930 the company launched what proved to be their most famous line, the *Alpha*

Bears, which came in gold or silver plush, and with their broad arms and stumpy legs have proved to be very sturdy. These bears are all labelled 'Farnell's ALPHA TOYS Made in England' and are valued at £400.

A second toymaker, **William J. Terry**, based in the East End of London, also began to make teddy bears just prior to the 1914–18 war. These bears, with their long, blond, silky mohair plush fur, were part of the company's *Terryer Toys* range and sold primarily through big stores in London and the other major cities. They are notable for the pronounced hump on their backs and a very appealing wide-eyed expression. Good examples, complete with the *Terryer* tag

A selection of mostly English teddy bears from the Twenties and Thirties.

(Left and opposite) Illustrations by Sylvia Wilgoss, chief designer of Dean's Rag Book Company, of the firm's top-selling teddy bears of the Twenties.

depicting a small terrier dog, can fetch in excess of £1,600.

Perhaps the best remembered English name to enter the market in the early days was **Dean's Rag Book Company**, founded in 1903 by the enterprising Henry S. Dean whose motto was to provide durable books for children 'who wear their food and eat their clothes'. Dean's launched the first of their delightful plush bears, with pointed ears and long jointed limbs, in 1914. These, complete with the firm's label showing two dogs attempting to tear apart one of Dean's rag books, are now worth up to £800. Later ranges included the *Evripose Bears* which, as their name implies, have jointed limbs that can be set in any position; and the *Colour Bears* which come in several shades from magenta to cream and have velvet pads and striking blue eyes. Both types of bear have been valued at between £500 and £600. In the 1930s Dean's also made a number of novelty bears, including printed cotton bears to cut out and make up, and a little chap on wheels which was sold with the instructions, 'He follows like a well-trained pet—all you have to do is pull the string'. Neither type has been seen for years and is therefore impossible to value.

Dean's continued to play a dominant role in the British teddy bear industry for years thereafter, moving to Rye in Sussex in the late 1950s, where they remained in business until 1982. During this era the company's chief designer, Silvia Willgoss—who kindly assisted me in the writing of the first edition of this book—produced a number of very collectable bears. She used the bears at London Zoo as one of her main sources of inspiration, and her 1955 range of white mohair bears with rubber paws and snout, which sit up exactly like

a real bear, are now eagerly sought after and can fetch up to £1,000 in fine condition.

With the benefit of hindsight, the First World War can be seen to have seriously undermined the German manufacturers' domination of the international teddy bear market. During those years they were unable to sell their products abroad and most factories were turned over to making items for the war. Nonetheless, the demand for bears remained, and although Britain was also involved in the conflict, several new firms sprang up to meet the need. Potential manufacturers were fortunate in having a ready supply of mohair plush fabric available from a group of weaving companies in Yorkshire, who were anxious to find an outlet for their product.

Although examples of the bears they made are now extremely rare, amongst those firms known to have been in business at this time were **The East London Toy Federation**, founded in 1914 by Sylvia Pankhurst, sister of the famous Suffragette leader, Emmeline; **Gray & Nicholls** of Liverpool whose *Mr Teddy* series, launched in 1915, proved very good at soothing wartime children; and the attractively named *Fondle Toys*, manufactured from 1917 onwards by Joseph Burman's **Zoo Toy Company**. This company also produced the unique *Teddy T* who, instead of a growler in his stomach, had an empty space which could be opened and used for storing small personal items. A Burman bear like this fetched £560

at auction recently.

Another novelty seen for the first time during the First World War were teddy bears dressed in patriotic uniforms. Many of these were produced by a London firm, **Harwin & Co.**, and designed by the owner's daughter, Dorothy. Called *Ally Bears*, the most popular figures were those dressed as British soldiers, sailors and Red Cross nurses. An *Ally Bear* kitted out as a Scottish soldier, complete with bonnet, kilt and sporran, was sold three years ago at Sotheby's for £3,000. The rarity of these bears has been attributed to the fact that many were bought for loved ones going to war, who never returned. However, a rare example is on show at the Museum of Childhood in Edinburgh.

With the coming of peace, English manufacturers went from strength to strength and another three new names joined the established favourites. They were **Chiltern Toys, Chad Valley** and **Merrythought**. All three have since become very collectable.

Interestingly, the story of **Chiltern Toys** begins with a German-born toymaker named Leon Rees who, since 1912, had been creating dolls at Chesham in his Chiltern Works, named

A century of bears! From left to right: King Skittle (1895); Steiff bear (1903); Schuco Yes No Bear (1923); Dean's Rag Book Co. Bear (1938); Chiltern Bear (1955); Mr Twisty (1966); Edgar (1995); Steiff 1908 Replica (1997). Photo: Roland Leon/ News Team International Ltd.

after the nearby range of hills. Rees had made his mark during the war with his *Mister Teddy*, a short plush bear with a wide grin, 'googly' eyes, pink-striped shirt and blue, patched trousers, who was based on a character featured in 'The Teddy Tail League', a comic strip for younger readers published in the *Daily Mail*. The bear is now very rare, and examples in anything like good condition are valued at £2,500. In 1920 Rees went into partnership with H. G. Stone and together they ran Chiltern Toys which rapidly became recognised as one of the most important makers of high-quality teddy bears because of their fine, soft mohair fur. The firm's products are also identifiable by their trademark showing a view of the Chiltern Hills and a label on each bear's right foot which reads 'Chiltern Hygienic Toys Made in England'. Among their most successful lines was *Baby Teddy* with his long pile coat, shaved muzzle and curved arms reinforced with wire so that they stretched out from his body. These delightful little bears in fine condition are worth around £500.

Chiltern Toys continued to prosper for the next forty years—even becoming one of the few firms to remain in production during the Second World War when they made a number of *Patriotic Bears*, including a Home Guard Sergeant complete with helmet (made of felt) whose value is now about £400—until 1967 when they were taken over by Chad Valley. Chiltern Bears, manufactured until 1978, are distinguished by their unique plastic noses (introduced in 1960 and in appearance rather more like a dog's muzzle than a bear's) and a label which states 'Chiltern Chad Valley'. They are, nonetheless, worth around £250 each.

Although **Chad Valley** itself did not begin full-time production of teddy bears until 1920, the company had actually been making toys since the end of the previous century when it was established in Birmingham. Their range of teddies made at Wellington in Shropshire had an immediate impact because of their bigger-than-normal size—some were 71 cm (28 ins) tall—as well as their golden mohair bodies and particularly soft limbs created by the use of kapok stuffing. The company made a point of this fact with a round stud in the bear's right ear embossed with the words 'Chad Valley AERO-LITE' to show what it contained. From 1938 to 1953 Chad Valley also promoted their Royal connection with a label displaying the Royal Crest and underneath the words 'By Appointment Toy Makers to HM The Queen'. (After 1953 this was altered to 'HM The Queen Mother'.) The most sought-after Chad Valley bears are those of the Thirties, which are valued at around £750 in fine condition.

In 1930 Chad Valley undertook the first of their two take-overs with the acquisition of **Peacock & Sons**, a firm based

in Clerkenwell, London, which had been making toys since 1853 and teddy bears from the early 1920s. Peacock's rather heavy-set, short plush mohair bears, with angular heads and heavy-set limbs, carry an embroidered red and white label on the right foot and have been valued at about £1,000. In time, however, Chad Valley went the same way as Chiltern Toys and Peacock & Sons when they themselves were taken over by Palitoy in 1980.

The last of the great English teddy bear makers who began operating in the Thirties were **Merrythought** who are still in business today and acknowledged as one of the oldest surviving British soft toy manufacturers. Indeed, in June 1990 the company made a special limited edition teddy, *Diamond Jubilee Bear*, who was similar to their original 1930s design with long, curved limbs, a small hump on his back and a pointed muzzle. He came complete with a royal blue ribbon round his neck and a numbered limited edition tag signed by the managing director, Oliver Holmes, the grandson of the firm's founder, W. G. Holmes.

W. G. Holmes had been a manufacturer of mohair with his partner, G. H. Laxton, when the two men sensed there might be a new outlet for their product and started producing teddy bears. They enlisted the expertise of C. R. Rendel who had worked for Chad Valley and A. C. Janisch of J. K. Farnell, and together the four men set up Merrythought Limited at Ironbridge in Shropshire. The firm's name was derived from the fact that Merrythought is an old English term for a 'forked bone' or wishbone, and this became their trademark. Their very first series of *Magnet Bears* carried a celluloid button embossed with the wishbone which was fixed to the bear's shoulder. It was later replaced by a label on the right paw.

For the first twenty years, Merrythought's chief designer was Florence Atwood, whose father had been a director of Chad Valley, and where she herself gained invaluable experience. An early star of the range was the long mohair plush *Sitting Bear Cub* which had large, floppy ears, curved arms and kapok filling which made it an ideal plaything for small children. Today such bears which have not been loved to death will command a price of about £750. A novel range of *Bingie Bears* also proved very popular, due to the colourful costumes in which they were dressed. They came in seven sizes, including two tiny versions for babies named *Baby Bingies*, and good examples can make £500 at auction.

However, probably the most successful design to come from Ironbridge was *Cheeky* who was born in 1957. With his long mohair fur, velvet nose, large amber and black eyes and broad grin, *Cheeky* proved irresistible. The bear was produced in a variety of sizes and versions; some wearing clothes, others

(Opposite) One of the most popular of English teddy bears, the Merrythought 'Cheeky', introduced in 1957.

129

with open mouths, but all containing a little bell in their right ear. If any more identification is needed, on the bottom of the right paw of every bear will be found the maker's label and the words 'Merrythought Ironbridge Shropshire Made in England Regd Design'. The value of these bears has skyrocketed in recent years and fine examples are valued at £500.

*   *   *

As I mentioned earlier, the First World War deprived German companies of their position as leaders in the manufacture of teddy bears. But once peace was restored in Europe, **Steiff**, **Schuco** and **Hermann** reorganised and were soon busy in the early Twenties producing new lines for the international marketplace.

Steiff particularly set their sights on the American market and introduced the *Teddy Clown* series of bears in eleven different sizes, ranging from 23 cm to 114 cm (9 ins to 45 ins) in height, with distinctive glass eyes and kapok stuffing for extra 'huggability'. The bears were made of mohair plush in brown, pink or gold and each one wore a ruff and white pierrot hat. Although vast numbers of *Teddy Clowns* were manufactured to meet demand, fine examples today can make anything up to £8,000. Another popular line from Steiff was *Teddy Baby* with pale golden plush mohair, a swivelling head and open mouth. Launched in 1929, the bear was designed to look like a real cub and, thanks to feet that were reinforced with cardboard, could be made to stand upright without support. This series was continued by Steiff until 1954, but it is still the pre-war models which have reached figures of £5,000 at auction. One exceptional example for this period was 'Edward T. Bear', a 1920 prototype two-tone yellow and brown mohair (known as a 'bicolour' by Steiff) which for a while held the world record auction price of £55,000. The bear, with his large rounded ears and unusually big brown glass eyes, was sold at Sotheby's in London in September 1989 to a Californian collector. It later transpired the man was determined to have the bear as an anniversary present for his wife, but when hearing what he had paid from his agent making the bids, he was said to be 'gobsmacked'.

The pride of the reopened **Hermann** factory was *Zotty*, a snub-nosed, shaggy mohair bear with a red ribbon and bell around his neck, who was based on a character from a popular series of German storybooks. One of these little individuals in good condition is now usually valued at £350. In 1930 the firm added several other distinctive smooth-haired small bears to the range and also changed the wording on their tags to 'Marke BEHA Teddy'. After the Second World War the

Hermann factory moved to Bamberg and from the early Fifties specialised in producing limited editions of their earlier bears, all labelled with the words 'Hermann Teddy Original'. (Make sure the word 'Teddy' is underlined as this is a sign of the bear's authenticity) and those bears which were produced in runs of less than 5,000 are now worth around £200.

Schuco continued to demonstrate their unrivalled expertise in the miniature bear range as well as introducing a new line of larger mohair bears in black and white, pink, purple and even green! These colourful teddies can fetch prices in excess of £600 when brought to auction. In the 1950s Schuco also produced for the United States a range of traditional bears with short plush coats, growlers and swivel-jointed bodies, which are valued at around £300 depending on their condition. Sadly, despite all their success with miniature teds, in the Seventies the company was unable to compete with cheaper products from Japan and went into bankruptcy.

Two of Steiff's most popular novelty bears: a 'Teddy Clown' and (*overleaf*) 'Teddy baby', both launched in the Twenties and sold for many years thereafter.

French toymakers also began to produce teddy bears in a serious way during the Twenties, despite the fact that dolls have always been much more popular with the country's children. Foremost among these were **M. Pintel Fils & Cie**, based in Paris. Their bears, like most others manufactured in France, are slimmer and straighter than their counterparts, made in brighter gold colours, and have shorter muzzles and hand-painted glass eyes. Pintel bears can be identified by a trade button carrying the maker's name on the ear or chest, and good examples can command £150 at auction. Where a number of French firms did excel at this time was with ingenious mechanical bears of which a number of fine examples still survive.

Other European countries to produce teddy bears in the years before and after the Second World War were Holland, Czechoslovakia and, especially, Austria where a range of stumpy, light brown bears with squat muzzles called *Heart Bears* produced by **Berg** in Vienna are now very collectable—in particular those made in the Fifties. These teddies are identifiable by a red bow, a heart-shaped badge hanging on their chests, and a label which reads 'Berg Tiere mit Hertz' (Berg Animals with Heart). Fine examples are worth up to £100.

On the other side of the world, Australia saw the arrival of its first 'home grown' teddies in 1920, when the husband and wife team of Joy and Gerald Kirby launched **Joy-Toys** in Melbourne. The company used sheepskin for its early models which were sometimes sold dressed in little suits and hats; later they produced a range of bears in honey-coloured mohair plush with flat, unjointed bodies and striking blue eyes. The most collectable bears are, however, those made from sheepskin with leather on their paws which are valued at £150. During its subsequent years Joy-Toys were given the franchise to produce a range of Walt Disney characters as toys and consequently made fewer teddies. In 1966 the company was taken over by Lines Brothers before eventually folding in the late Seventies. In neighbouring Japan, 'novelty bears' were also manufactured from the Thirties onwards, although as they were generally made from blanket wool and had external joints, their life span was often short and their value today not much more than £25.

Three more companies emerged in the Thirties—two in America and one in England—which were destined to become major players: the **Gund Manufacturing Company** of New York, **The Character Toy Company** in Connecticut and **Pedigree Soft Toys** of Merton in Surrey.

A German émigré named Adolph Gund set up the toymaking firm that bore his name in Norwalk, Connecticut, in the year 1898. However, it was not until a quarter of a century later, after the company had relocated to New York, that it commenced making teddy bears. These traditional humped-back, long-limbed bears in dark brown silk plush are now valued at £200. The firm was subsequently taken over by one of Gund's partners, but still carries his name and continues to satisfy the demand for old-fashioned and limited edition bears.

The Character Toy Company, as its name suggests, set out to produce bears that were very individual. Although it is fair to observe that some of the early models are rather like those of Steiff with their long limbs and pointed muzzles—and the firm did copy the German idea of inserting an identification tag in the ears of their bears—what ensured success was a later range of increasingly stylised bears with broad grins and jointed limbs that a child could move into any position. The early, brown bears can fetch around £200 at auction, while fine examples of the more versatile and unusual 'characters' of the Forties may make double this figure.

Lines Brothers Ltd, for many years Britain's biggest and most successful toy company, formed **Pedigree Soft Toys** as a subsidiary in the Thirties. In 1937 they started making teddy bears at Lines' Tri-ang Works in Merton. These cheerful-looking brown plush bears with their rounded heads, very slight muzzle, glass eyes and velvet pads soon became known as 'the teddies of childhood' and proved so popular that in 1946 Pedigree opened another factory in Belfast to keep pace with demand. Whether manufactured in Surrey or Northern Ireland, all the bears carry a blue label with the word Pedigree and the source of manufacture. The company remained a major supplier of teddy bears in the United Kingdom for over half a century, despite successive take-overs in 1966 by Rovex Industries and in 1972 by Dunbee-Combex-Marx, before going out of business in 1988. Bears from its heyday in the Forties and Fifties sell for between £50 to £200 depending on age and condition.

Like the First World War, the 1939–45 conflict disrupted the making of teddy bears. But again in its aftermath most of the leading companies in Britain, Europe and America returned to production, although it is true to say that sales in the Fifties and Sixties never reached the same levels as those during the inter-war years. The development of several new artificial materials, including nylon plush and cotton rayon, plastic eyes and rust-proof wire, resulted in various lines of 'safety' bears appearing on the market to comply with the increasing number of safety standards introduced by government. The most famous of these new-style bears were those made by **Wendy Boston**, a company formed by

Ken and Wendy (née Boston) Williams in Wales, who introduced their cuddly, unjointed, kapok-filled *Playsafe* bears in 1948.

The Welsh firm's major achievement, however, was to use artificial fabrics and plastic eyes and thereby create the very first machine-washable teddy. Older readers may remember that traumatic evening in 1955 when a demonstrator on television showed how a dirty bear could be made sparkling clean by a dip in a washing machine and then a wring-out in the mangle! To add insult to injury, the bear was hung out to dry by his ears! This shameful period in teddy bear history, when it became almost commonplace to see bears draped from washing lines among the clothes and sheets, deserves to have a decent veil drawn across it! Wendy Boston was taken over in 1968 by another toymaker, Denys Fisher. Meanwhile, those *Playsafe* bears which survived their ordeal by water are now valued at between £30–£50.*

It was not only the materials from which bears were made that changed—their characters also underwent a radical revision. In England in 1967, for example, **Dean's** introduced *Scenty Bear* who was perfumed to help children get to sleep, while **Chad Valley** offered *Talking Teddy* who recited comforting words when a cord attached to his back was pulled. Versions of both these types have sold for up to £50 in recent years.

Still among the most collectable bears of this period are those made by **Steiff**—especially the limited edition *Jackie Bear* produced to mark the firm's half-century in 1953. He looked just like a bear cub, came in three different sizes and was sold with a label celebrating the teddy bear's fiftieth birthday. These bears are worth in excess of £500. The company also made a line of *Nimrod Bears* which came in four different colours and were dressed to look like a traditional German huntsman with hat, felt tunic and a wooden rifle in one paw. Fine examples have been sold for £350. Also in the Sixties, Steiff produced their own version of the chubby storybook character *Zotty*, with thick, shaggy brown coat, open mouth and a yellow ribbon around his neck. This bear, again, is valued at about £300. Since then the company has

---

* If you *must* wash a teddy bear, for whatever reason, let me give you some tried and tested advice. Most should never be put in a washing machine as this can be disastrous, but should be hand-washed and rinsed and hung out in a plastic net bag until dry. Small bears may be spin-dried, but *never* hang any teddy out to dry by his ears as this can damage the material. Net bags should be easily obtainable from your nearest friendly greengrocer.

continued to create modern versions of its original bears in various sizes, to the delight of collectors all over the world.

Quality bears were also the hallmark of another German company, **Grisly Spielwaren Fabrik**, founded in 1954 at Kirchheimbolamdern by Karl Unfricht, a man who had loved teddy bears since his childhood. Unfricht's lines are known as *Grisly Bears* and are made of acrylic plush and dralon in either light brown or dark brown colours. They have an easy-to-spot button on their chests which shows a bear on all fours, a needle and thread, and the word 'Grisly'. The special edition of 1,000 *Original Grisly Bears,* issued in 1984, are now fetching over £100 at auction.

In America, the well-known soft toy manufacturer **R. Dakin** inadvertently entered the teddy bear market in 1957 when it received a shipment of model trains from Japan around which had been packed a number of inexpensive teddy bears to prevent damage in transit. When a member of the Dakin family saw this 'ballast' he decided the bears were actually attractive enough to sell. The immigrants proved so popular that in a short while teddy bears became the company's most successful line. Dakin is particularly noted for setting the highest safety standards by ensuring that no toxic materials are used in the manufacture of its bears, and the eyes go through rigorous tests to ensure they are firmly fixed and safe. The company's most successful line in recent years has been *Pooky,* modelled on the bear that is featured in the strip cartoon adventures of Garfield the cat.

An English firm which has also had a considerable impact is **The House of Nisbet**. Established in 1953 by Jack Wilson to make dolls, the company added teddy bears to its lines in 1978 and these have become a firm favourite with collectors. In 1980 Jack's daughter, Alison, designed *Bully Bear,* based on a bear in Peter Bull's famous collection, and the bear and his owner were the star attractions at the launching party in the House of Commons for the first edition of this book. Early examples in good condition have now doubled in value from the original price. *Bully Bear* was, in fact, very similar to Peter Bull's much-travelled 'Delicatessen', who is believed to be a 1907 Ideal Toy Company bear and was given to the actor in 1970 by a viewer who saw him on the Johnny Carson TV show in America. In 1987 'Delicatessen' became even more famous when he starred on television as Sebastian Flyte's bear, 'Aloysius', in Granada TV's outstanding dramatisation of *Brideshead Revisited* by Evelyn Waugh.

Jack Wilson was so impressed by the bear's performance that he produced a replica in distressed mohair plush with chamois leather patches on its limbs and body. The bear was also fashionably dressed in a Daks Simpson scarf, carried a

(Opposite) The House of Nisbet's 'Bully Bear', based on Peter Bull's much-loved teddy.

136

British Airways flight bag, and had a woven label with his name and the House of Nisbet's trademark of two bears holding a shield on its right foot. Wilson wanted to call the teddy 'Aloysius', but as the copyright had already been sold to an American firm, **The North American Bear Company**, he settled for the original name; of the two bears, 'Delicatessen' is now generally considered to be the more valuable.

In recent years an increasing number of small companies and individuals have begun making their own unique style of teddy bears, and only time will tell which ones will become the most sought after and valuable. Among those which I have seen that I would recommend for their quality and originality are Joan and Maude Blackburn's traditional **Canterbury Bears** made in the Kent town of that name; Susan and David Rixon's **Nonsuch Soft Toys** based in Berkshire; and, from America, the lovely limited edition antique teddies produced by **Sue Foskey** in Delaware, New Jersey.

If any more evidence is required of the extraordinary growth of this bearish market, then let me just note the success story of Jonty and Alice Crossick whose **English Teddy Bear Company**, based in Bath, recently raised venture capital to expand their business in Japan, the rest of Asia and America. The Crossicks, who met at university where they first had the idea of opening a shop to sell handmade bears and accessories, have since 1991 opened eleven shops based in popular British tourist localities, including Cambridge, Bath and London, attracting visitors and British collectors as well. The couple's success has been summed up in these words by Jonty which I heartily echo: 'We knew teddy bears were a good way to get a message of fun across to people.'

(*Opposite*) Delicatessen, Peter Bull's teddy, who became 'Aloysius' in the Granada TV dramatisation of *Brideshead Revisited*. The bear, seen here with Anthony Andrews, has since been replicated for sale to admirers by the North American Bear Company.

12

THE BEAR FACTS

Here are some useful addresses and sources of information for those readers who are new to the appeal of teddy bears and may like to learn more about them and the world of arctophiles.

TEDDY BEAR MUSEUMS

The Bear Museum
38 Dragon Street,
Petersfield, Hampshire
GU31 4JJ.
Tel: 01730 65108

Bethnal Green Museum of Childhood
Cambridge Heath Road,
Bethnal Green, London
E2 9PA.
Tel: 0181 981 1711

Bournemouth Bears: The Dorset Teddy Bear Museum
Old Christchurch Lane,
Bournemouth BN4 6FC.
Tel: 01202 293544

London Toy and Model Museum
21–23 Craven Hill, London
W2 3EN.
Tel: 0171 262 9450

Merrythought Shop and Museum
Dale End, Ironbridge,
Telford, Shropshire TF8 7NJ.
Tel: 01952 433019

Museum of Childhood
42 High Street, Edinburgh
EH1 1TG.
Tel: 0131 225 2424

National Toy Museum
The Grange, The Green,
Rottingdean, East Sussex
BN2 7HA
Tel: 01273 301004

Pollock's Toy Museum
1 Scala Street, London
W1P 1LT.
Tel: 0171 636 3452

Rom's Bazaar and Museum
2 Badgery's Crescent,
Lawson 2783, Australia.

The Steiff Museum
Alleenstrasse 2, D-7928,
Giengen (Brenz), Germany.

The Teddy Bear Museum
19 Greenhill Street,
Stratford-upon-Avon,
Warwickshire CV37 6LF.

Irena Thompson's Toy and Teddy Bear Museum
373 Clifton Drive North,
St Anne's, Lytham St Anne's,
Lancashire FY8 2PA.
Tel: 01253 713705

The Margaret Woodbury Strong Museum
Rochester, New York, USA.

TEDDY BEAR MAGAZINES

Bear Collector
Avalon Court, Star Road,
Partridge Green,
West Sussex RH13 8RY.
Tel: 01403 711511

Teddy Bear and Friends Magazine
Hobby House Press, Inc.,
900 Frederick Street,
Cumberland,
Maryland 21502, USA.
Tel: 00 1 (301) 759 5853

Teddy Bear Scene
The Old Barn,
Ferringham Lane, Ferring,
West Sussex BN12 5LL.
Tel: 01903 506626

The Teddy Bear Club International Magazine
Maze Media Ltd,
Castle House, 97 High Street,
Colchester, Essex CO1 1TH.
Tel: 01206 563363

Teddy Bear Times
Avalon Court, Star Road,
Partridge Green,
West Sussex RH13 8RY.
Tel: 01403 711511

TEDDY BEAR CHARITIES

Good Bears of the World (UK) Trust
Chairman: Mrs Audrey
Duck, 256 St Margaret's
Road, Twickenham,
Middlesex TW1 1PR.
Tel: 0181 891 5746

Good Bears of the World (USA)
Chairman: Mrs Terrie Stong,
PO Box 13097, Toledo,
Ohio 43613, USA.
Tel: 00 1 (419) 531 5365

TEDDY BEAR CLUBS

British Bear Club
Avalon Court, Star Road,
Partridge Green,
West Sussex RH13 8RY.

British Teddy Bear Association
PO Box 290, Brighton,
West Sussex BN2 1DR.
Tel: 01273 697974

The Dean's Collectors Club
Pontypool, Gwent NP4 6YY.

Address for American residents
c/o Hobby House Press, Inc.,
1 Corporate Drive,
Grantsville, MD 21536.

The Followers of Rupert
5 Long Meadow, Markyate,
St Albans, Hertfordshire
AL3 8JW.
Tel: 01582 841266

Holmfirth Bears Fan Club
S. Whitcomb, 68 Leeds Road
Oulton, Leeds LS26 8JY.

International League of Teddy Bear Collectors Club
1023 Don Diablo, Arcadia,
California 91006, USA.
Tel: 00 1 (818) 447 3809

Japan Teddy Bear Association
Komatsu-Bldg, 16–20,
Nanpeidai-chou Shibuya-ku,
Tokyo 150, Japan.

Japan Teddy Bear Fan Club
2–16–202 Uchido-cho,
Ashiya-City Hyogo 659,
Japan.

Paddington's Action Club
Vincent House,
Springfield Road, Horsham,
West Sussex RH12 2PN.
Tel: 01403 210406

Steiff Club (UK Office)
69–71 High Street, Epsom,
Surrey KT19 8DH.
Tel: 01372 745007

Teddy Bears' Picnick
Kostverlorenpad 1b,
PO Box 333, 3960 BH Wijk
bij Duurstede,
The Netherlands.
Tel: 00 31 343 578716

Teddy Ecosse
The Wynd, Melrose,
Roxburghshire,
Scotland TD6 9PA.

Teddy's Patch
Le Club des Amis de l'Ours,
34 rue Lieu de Sante,
76000 Rouen, France.
Tel: 00 33 88 96 00

SELECTED RETAILERS

The Bear Shop
18 Elm Hill, Norwich,
Norfolk NR3 1HN.
Tel: 01603 766866

Budleigh Bears
28 Fore Street,
Budleigh Salterton,
Devon EX9 6NH.
Tel: 01395 443641

Classic Teddy Bears
Colombo Court 01–15,
Singapore 179742.
Tel: 00 65 3375438

Clemens Bears of Germany
21 The Grange, Ashgate,
Chesterfield,
Derbyshire S42 7PS.
Tel: 01246 567900

Cotswold Bears
Fern Dairy Farm, Manor
Lane, Little Comberton,
Pershore, Worcestershire
WR10 3ER.
Tel: 01386 710721

The English Teddy Bear Company
Selected shops:

8 Abbey Churchyard,
Bath BA1 1LY.
Tel: 01225 338655

1 King's Parade,
Cambridge CB2 1SJ.
Tel: 01223 300908

4 St Peter's Street,
Canterbury CT1 2AD.
Tel: 01227 784640

42 Piccadilly,
London W1V 9AJ.
TEl: 0171 491 2091
(*Other London shops in Regent Street and Carnaby Street.*)

135 High Street,
Oxford OX1 4DN.
Tel: 01865 721165

47 High Street, Windsor,
Berkshire SL4 1LR.
Tel: 01753 862524

36 Stonegate,
York YO1 2AS.
Tel: 01904 622822

(*The English Teddy Bear Company also has shops in Newcastle and Stratford-upon-Avon.*)

Growlies
15 Thorn Brae, Johnstone,
Scotland PA5 8HF.
Tel: 015053 36551

Hermann Teddy Original
1 Georgian Close,
Gordon Avenue, Stanmore,
Middlesex HA7 3QT.
Tel: 0181 954 5956

Heritage Bears
Greenbanks, Yew Tree Farm,
Molesworth, Cambridgeshire
PE18 0QD.
Tel: 01832 710622

The Old Bear Company
PO Box 29, Chesterfield,
Derbyshire S42 5YY.
Tel: 01246 850446

Pinocchio
79 High Street, Teddington,
Middlesex TW11 8HG.
Tel: 0181 977 8995

Teddy Bears of Witney
99 High Street, Witney,
Oxfordshire OX8 6LY.
Tel: 01999 702616

The Rupert Wallace Teddy Bear Shop
62A Victoria Street,
Glossop, Derbyshire.
Tel: 01457 857451

ACKNOWLEDGEMENTS

I would like to express my gratitude to my husband, Peter, who helped me in the writing of the original book but has modestly withdrawn his name from this completely revised new edition. Although they are no longer with us, I am still deeply indebted to Colonel Bob Henderson, Peter Bull and Jim Ownby whose generous advice and access to their files made the first book possible. Among other individuals whom I should like to thank are Mark Michtom of the former Ideal Toy Corporation, I.A. Schmeizl of Margarete Steiff GmbH, W.O.G.Lofts, Jean Eaton Warren, Audrey Duck, Herbert R. Collins, Judith Robbins, Denis Gifford, Patrick Matthews, Mike Young, Lucy Rigg, Stewart Ferguson and Michael Bond. Acknowledgement is also due to the following organisations and newspapers for allowing copyright material to be reproduced in this new edition: *Sunday Express*, *The Independent*/ Philip Meech, *Daily Mail*, Peter Trievnor/Times Newspapers Ltd., *Daily Express*, *Radio Times*, *The People*, the People, *Punch*, *Life*, *Art & Antiques Magazine*, *Playthings*, *The Veterinary Record*, *Bear Tracks*, D.C. Thomson Ltd, Western Publishing Corporation, Fleetway Publications, HarperCollins Ltd., Methuen Ltd., The Swiss Tourist Office, Express News & Features Service, Syndication International, Keystone Picture Agency, Roland Leon/News Team International, Dean's Childsplay Toys, Merrythought Ltd., The British Film Institute, Campione Fine Art, Sotheby's and Christie's Images. Finally, the staffs of the London Library, the British Museum, the National Portrait Gallery, the Library of Congress and the Smithsonian Institution who helped locate a great deal of research material – and, of course, those arctophiles whose memories of their teddy bears were a constant source of inspiration, especially Jonna Koster of the Netherlands who turned my publisher on to the idea of the book long before the subject had become the international phenomenon it is today.

Philippa Waring
July 1997